THE LITTLE LEAGUE THAT COULD

THE
LITTLE LEAGUE
THAT COULD

A HISTORY OF THE AMERICAN FOOTBALL LEAGUE

KEN RAPPOPORT

TAYLOR TRADE PUBLISHING
Lanham • New York • Boulder • Toronto • Plymouth, UK

Published by Taylor Trade Publishing
An imprint of The Rowman & Littlefield Publishing Group, Inc.
4501 Forbes Boulevard, Suite 200, Lanham, Maryland 20706
http://www.rlpgtrade.com

Estover Road, Plymouth PL6 7PY, United Kingdom

Distributed by National Book Network

British Library Cataloguing in Publication Information Available

Library of Congress Cataloging-in-Publication Data Available

Rappoport, Ken.
 The little league that could : a history of the American Football League / Ken Rappoport.
  p.   cm.
 Includes index.
 ISBN 978-1-58979-462-7 (cloth : alk. paper) — ISBN 978-1-58979-463-4 (electronic)
 1. American Football League—History. I. Title.
 GV955.5.A45R36 2010
 796.332'640973—dc22

                                                              2010005837

 ∞ The paper used in this publication meets the minimum requirements of American
National Standard for Information Sciences—Permanence of Paper for Printed Library
Materials, ANSI/NISO Z39.48-1992.

Printed in the United States of America

To those who believed,
and those who still remember the AFL.

Contents

Acknowledgments

No one can do a book alone, and this is most certainly the case with *The Little League That Could*. First and foremost, I must thank Barry Wilner for his input. I am most grateful for his expertise in the preparation of this book.

Nor could the story of the AFL be told without input from dozens of people who graciously shared their recollections.

Heartfelt thanks go out to Jack Steadman, who was there at the start with Lamar Hunt when the idea of a new league took shape. And thanks also to Barron Hilton, the original owner of the Chargers whose franchise was one of the linchpins of the little league that dared to stand up to the established NFL in a true David-versus-Goliath test.

Norma Hunt, Lamar Hunt's widow, shared personal stories, as did her son, Clark.

I am grateful also to Patrick Sullivan, son of the Patriots' original owner, Billy Sullivan, for insights into his father. And to Al Locasale, a longtime personnel director with the Raiders. Thanks also to Art Modell, longtime owner of the Cleveland Browns, and Mike Brown, son of football legend Paul Brown.

The following players were also kind enough to share their recollections of a different time in American sports:

Larry Eisenhauer, Ron Mix, Billy Shaw, George Saimes, Ed Rutkowski, Booker Edgerson, Elbert Dubenion, Jon Morris, Larry Garron, Len Dawson, Lance Alworth, Norm Evans, Bob Johnson, Tommy Brooker, Larry Grantham, Lionel Taylor, and Willie West.

Thanks also go out to Ed Abramoski, Ron Hobson, Gil Santos, Ange Coniglio, Gerald Eskenazi, Scott Berchtold, Gil Brandt, Jack Brennan, Joe Browne, Harvey Greene, Joe Horrigan, Stacey James, Bill Johnston, Frank Ramos, Jim Saccomano, Teresa M. Walker, and John Wawrow.

Prologue

I magine:

No Super Bowl.

No Monday Night Football.

No national TV contract for the NFL and no shared revenues.

Without Lamar Hunt, longtime owner of the Kansas City Chiefs, what would pro football be like today?

"Think about it," said Hall of Fame quarterback Len Dawson. "No American Football League, no merger with the National Football League."

And none of the innovations that are so familiar to fans of today's game, such as the two-point conversion, player identification on uniforms, or official time on the scoreboard clocks.

"Lamar was a visionary," said Jack Steadman, the longtime top executive with the Kansas City Chiefs who worked with Hunt to help form the AFL in 1960. "Without question, Lamar held the league together until the merger and then was the principal one to negotiate the merger with the NFL."

With Hunt one of the driving forces, the AFL challenged the NFL's dominance in professional football. In head-to-head competition for players and the sport's public affection, the AFL more than held its own for 10 seasons from 1960 through 1969. Along the way, the competing leagues merged, changing the face of football forever.

No AFL teams folded, and only two teams changed cities during the league's 10-year existence.

A far cry from other leagues that had challenged the NFL, which had been in existence since 1920, when it was known as the American Professional Football Association.

In three different decades—the 1920s, 1930s, and 1940s—a league calling itself the AFL tried to make a go of it against the entrenched NFL. All failed.

The All America Football Conference was another pretender and would last only four years before it had three teams absorbed by the NFL.

In later years, the United States Football League and the World Football League would add their names to leagues that had failed to successfully challenge the NFL.

But none had the staying power of the 1960s version of the AFL, which had the resources, talent, and drive to challenge the lordly NFL.

Same game of football, more flair.

"That was the ID of the AFL, that it was wide-open football, throw it any place, anywhere, and any time," said defensive back Willie West, who played for St. Louis in the NFL before hooking up with Buffalo, Denver, New York, and Miami in the AFL.

"Offenses were geared to scoring bunches of points, so they did lots of passing. And it was almost all medium-range to deep passes. The deep pass at that time was really the most relied-upon offensive play in the AFL."

The fourth AFL had flash and dash.

With gunslinging quarterbacks such as John Hadl, Joe Namath, George Blanda, Len Dawson, Jack Kemp, Babe Parilli, and Daryle Lamonica throwing their "bombs," high-scoring games were the norm.

Sid Gillman, who coached the high-powered Hadl–to–Lance Alworth combination at San Diego, was largely responsible for moving the passing game to soaring new heights.

A telling statistic: In every season of the AFL's 10-year history, the league posted a higher average than the NFL of passes thrown per team, and it wasn't even close.

In 1968, the NFL seemed to be living up to its image as a conservative running league when its teams averaged but 192 passes for the season. By comparison, AFL teams averaged a staggering 404.

The AFL's image as a high-powered offensive league wasn't a myth. Comparing the two leagues, AFL teams had the three highest point totals in any of the 10 seasons: Houston in 1961 with 513 points and the Oakland Raiders with 468 in 1967 and 453 in 1968.

Another telling stat: In seven of the 10 seasons that the two leagues existed simultaneously, the AFL averaged more touchdown passes per season. And in nine seasons, the AFL outdistanced the NFL in total passing yardage per team.

Not that the NFL was totally inefficient in the passing game. In fact, NFL quarterbacks posted a higher completion percentage than their AFL counterparts every season of the 10-year period. Another startling stat: NFL passers completed better than 50 percent of their pass attempts every year, while AFL quarterbacks never had a season with more than 50 percent pass completions.

The AFL, though, continued to draw attention to itself with its flashy, pass-oriented attacks.

The league made sure that millions of fans across the country saw them fill the air with footballs. They put all of their regular-season games on network TV, another football first. With 14 season games, two more than the NFL, the AFL had plenty of action to show.

What were Sunday afternoons without the professional tones of Curt Gowdy calling plays of an AFL game on national television? Gowdy's presence brought legitimacy to the AFL and brought new fans to the league.

Growing out of this was yet another innovation: shared television and gate receipts among the teams. AFL franchises were truly in the money now.

And because the AFL was looking for talent wherever it could find it, the door was opened wider for athletes from historically black small colleges. Certainly the NFL had some blacks on rosters but was generally a conservative, white-dominated league.

By the mid-1960s, blacks could boast a total of 22 representatives in the 1964 AFL All-Star Game. And they made their presence felt in other ways, boycotting the All-Star Game in New Orleans that year because of what they considered unfair treatment of blacks in the Crescent City. The game was shifted to Houston, where the West team beat the East 38–14.

By the time the AFL had finished its tenth season in 1969, it had a firm grip on America's consciousness and a place in the NFL. And by 1970, the leagues were divided into the National Conference and American Conference and started to play an interleague schedule.

By then, the Super Bowl had become a fixture in American sports, a virtual American holiday. And the light of television was showing the way.

Hunt had an inkling television would be a big-league partner with football, particularly after watching the exciting 1958 New York Giants–Baltimore Colts playoff game to decide the NFL title. Hunt was one of some 45 million fans across the nation to do so.

"Lamar was convinced from watching that game that football was the best sport for television, and he just envisioned that football would become very big because of television," Steadman said.

When Hunt's Kansas City Chiefs played the Green Bay Packers in the first championship game between the AFL and NFL, it wasn't called the Super Bowl—just the "AFL-NFL World Championship Game."

"Then it was that spring that Lamar had the vision that it's the 'Super Bowl,'" Steadman said. "[NFL commissioner Pete] Rozelle really fought it. He just didn't think it was right at all, and he continued to call it the World Championship Game. But the press had picked up the 'Super Bowl,' and from then on, the media just referred to it as the 'Super Bowl.'"

Apropos, the AFL's impact on football came in a time of great change in America.

From the man in the White House to the man on the moon, the 1960s were one of the most dramatic decades in American history and also one of its most tragic, with the assassinations of President Kennedy, Robert Kennedy, and Martin Luther King Jr.

A cry for civil rights echoed in the black communities across the country. President Johnson, who replaced Kennedy in the White House, answered these cries by signing the Civil Rights Act. But the African Americans' battle for civil rights was just beginning, as riots, sit-ins, and Black Power movements raged across the country and blacks marched on Washington.

While doors were still being closed to blacks in many parts of American society, the AFL was opening them—at least to a larger degree than the NFL.

"The truth is, organized athletics has done more to bring races and religions together than just about any other activity or organizations in the United States," notes Ron Mix, an all-star lineman with the Chargers. "The participants, even if they hadn't been exposed to other races and religions, once they see everyone is the same, their minds change. Fans suddenly find themselves rooting for black players, and whether they know it or not, slowly over time their minds change."

Other movements were prominent in America.

With the escalation of the Vietnam War, peaceniks put out a call to bring U.S. soldiers home. Once again, Americans marched on Washington.

The feminists, meanwhile, were involved in their own revolution for women's rights that eventually made its own kind of history.

Nearing the end of the 1960s, America had something to be proud of by landing a man on the moon.

Neil Armstrong's "one giant leap for mankind" not only was that, but it also put America back on top in the space race.

And, by the way, during the same decade a renegade sports league managed to change the face of football. The AFL became the first pro football league to successfully challenge the NFL.

Here, then, is the story of a long uphill fight by a football league that was impossible to bring down and the fascinating people, places, and events that were part of that story.

1

Challenging Goliath

Lamar Hunt was frustrated.

For most of his life, the Texas oil millionaire dreamed of bringing a football team to Dallas. But Hunt was stopped at the goal line—the NFL said, "No!"

What does a Texas oil millionaire do when he is rejected?

Easy. He starts a league of his own.

Welcome, American Football League.

Welcome, "Foolish Club."

Foolish Club. Why foolish?

That's what the owners of the new league called themselves. The name was attributed to Wayne Valley, one of the owners of the Oakland franchise.

"He felt that anybody was foolish if he wanted to be with the AFL and invest in a new franchise," said Barron Hilton, owner of the Los Angeles Chargers and scion of the royal hotel family. "And then Wayne joined."

Hunt was determined to make the new league work. He counted on his team in Dallas to be one of the linchpins of the operation.

Hunt had zealous faith in his idea. Two years before, he had watched the NFL's championship game between the New York Giants and Baltimore Colts on television. He was transfixed by the compelling back and forth action on his TV screen. He was convinced that pro football would become very popular because of television.

But not even the visionary Hunt could know how big.

"He was the key to putting the deal together, putting the group together, and holding it together," said Jack Steadman, Hunt's long-time top executive.

One of 15 children of Texas oil baron H. L. Hunt, one of the richest men in the world, Lamar Hunt earned the nickname "Games" because of his love of sports. He captained the football team at a private boys' prep school in Pennsylvania. When he went off to college at Southern Methodist University (SMU), Lamar hoped to play football. He did, but just barely, riding the pines as a third-stringer.

His athletic skills soon took a backseat to his prowess as a student and, eventually, his entrepreneurial skills.

It took a while.

"When Lamar graduated from SMU, they were looking for something for him to do in the oil business," Steadman said. "He had no interest in it, but they made him the managing partner of a drilling company."

It would seem Steadman and Hunt were destined to meet and collaborate. Like Hunt, Steadman had gone to SMU. Hunt studied geology, while Steadman graduated with a BA in business administration.

Steadman was working for the Hunt Oil Company when Lamar took over the drilling division. That's when the two first met, unaware that their association would take them to historic heights in the world of sports.

"I would have to get him to sign some legal documents on occasion," Steadman remembered. "I basically got to know him, but not too well. It was just a quick business relationship."

Hunt wasn't interested as much in oil as he was in football. In the late 1950s, Hunt had been thinking about getting into professional football as an owner. Two options came to mind: buying a current NFL team or starting an expansion team.

Hunt went after both options.

He met with NFL commissioner Bert Bell to inquire about a possible expansion franchise for Dallas. Bell told him that the NFL was not going to expand. There was word, though, about the possibility that the Chicago Cardinals might be available for the right buyer. The Cardinals were in a tug-of-war with the Chicago Bears for city supremacy,

Hunt wasted no time getting to Chicago to negotiate with Cardinals owner Violet Wolfner. She was the widow of Charles Bidwill, the Cardinals' original owner, now married to Walter Wolfner.

Hunt wasn't the only moneyed Texas oilman interested in buying the Cardinals. Houston's Bud Adams was, too.

"Violet Wolfner didn't want to sell more than 49 percent and the deal fell through," Adams told *Sports Illustrated* in a 1960 interview.

Hunt, meanwhile, had spent a lot of hours negotiating with Wolfner, with the same result.

"At one time he was pretty close to buying the Cardinals," Steadman said.

The Wolfners finally decided to move the Cardinals to St. Louis instead of selling the team.

Shut out twice. What to do?

At some point during his travels, a frustrated Hunt gave weight to a crazy, long-shot idea. On his way through Houston, he stopped by to see Adams.

"I didn't know him but we had dinner together, and in the course of the conversation we reminisced about buying the Cardinals," Adams said. "Just before he left for the airport I told Lamar, 'Maybe we ought to start our own league.'"

That's just what Hunt was thinking.

"The next time I saw him, maybe three months later, he had lined up four other franchises besides his hometown Dallas club and asked me if I wanted in," Adams said. "I said, 'Hell, yes.'"

Hunt brought Steadman in as his top business associate. Steadman was surprised when Hunt told him he had big plans for a new football league and asked him to set up the league office in Dallas.

"For some reason I'll never know, he was impressed with me," Steadman said. "It was the first time I had done anything like that. I did the research and set up the league offices of the American Football League.

"Then I set up the business operation for the Dallas Texans for Lamar, and I did all this while I was with the drilling company. And then after that, he asked me to come on full-time. So I was kind of there with him from the beginning."

Hunt's first four city choices along with his own were Houston, Denver, Minneapolis, and Seattle. He especially wanted Houston because of the potential of a Texas rivalry. Hunt also felt that it wouldn't be a major league without Los Angeles and New York.

Welcome Hilton in Los Angeles and Harry Wismer, a well-known sports broadcaster, in the Big Apple.

Hilton was at his office on Sunset Boulevard in Hollywood when Hunt called and asked for a meeting.

"Lamar came out," Hilton recalled. "I had never met him before. He told me about his efforts to get an NFL club and also that Bud Adams was trying to get one. They decided they would start their own league. They asked if I'd be interested in having the Los Angeles franchise."

Hilton jumped at the opportunity.

"One of the reasons I became involved was that my mother's second husband was a coach at the College of Mines in El Paso," Hilton said.

"I used to sit on the sideline every once in a while when he was coaching. It kind of excited me, pro football especially. [Los Angeles Rams owners] Dan Reeves and Ed Pauley were good friends of mine. I don't think they liked the idea of my starting a team for the AFL in LA. Their desire was for us to go away. We had some interesting interviews back and forth with each other. I was telling them the AFL was here to stay, and I don't think they wanted to hear that."

While Hunt was dedicated to the success of the new league, there were reasons for concern, especially with the NFL's sudden reversal of field.

"As soon as Lamar announced the start of the league, then the NFL expanded," Steadman said. "They decided they were going to put a team on top of the AFL's Dallas franchise. They were going to take on Lamar."

So the NFL awarded the Cowboys to Clint Murchison, a business rival of Hunt's. The Hunts and Murchisons were the two prominent families in Dallas at the time, both in oil. So that not only started a war between the AFL and NFL but also started a business war in Dallas. Lamar was trying to line up the business people whom he dealt with to support the Texans, and Murchison was doing the same with the Cowboys.

The NFL had taken off the gloves and delivered a body blow to the upstart league. For the time being, Hunt and his pals had to shrug off the blindside hit by the NFL and take care of their own business.

It was war, football style. And like all wars, there was intrigue, subterfuge, and a battle plan.

The NFL had fired the first shot and made a direct hit on its target by placing a team in Dallas. No question, the NFL wished to sink the new league that had been originally formed with teams in New York, Dallas, Denver, Houston, Los Angeles, and Minneapolis–St. Paul.

In making the announcement of the league to the media in the summer of 1959, Hunt mentioned the possibility of adding two more teams.

The *New York Times* reported that Hunt "foresees a possible expansion to eight teams, with the additional two coming from Seattle, Buffalo, San Francisco, Miami, Kansas City, or New Orleans." Seattle was soon ruled out because it didn't have a stadium. In another story, San Diego, Louisville, and the Canadian city of Vancouver were also reportedly in the hunt for a franchise.

The AFL plan was to play 14 games with four exhibition games. At the time, NFL teams played 12 league games and six exhibitions.

The AFL planned to one-up the NFL not only in regular-season games but also in salaries: the minimum salary for players in the new league would be 10 percent higher than the NFL, which paid $6,500 per season. The AFL would also pay officials "substantially more than in the NFL, which was said to have $3,000 per season as the highest salary," the *New York Times* reported.

Going into the fall of 1959, the AFL still sought to add two teams to make it an eight-team league before its draft to stock rosters in November. First Buffalo came on board, owned by a group headed by Ralph Wilson. Then Billy Sullivan's Boston team a month later, on the eve of the draft, was the last piece of the puzzle.

So the eight-team league was all set to pick players for its rosters, many of them from the college ranks. Or was it?

There were rumors that the Minneapolis–St. Paul club, spearheaded by Max Winter, was going to pull out and join the NFL at the final hour.

Hilton got Winter on the phone.

"I called Max the night before the draft and said, 'Max, there is a rumor you are going into the NFL.' He said, 'Oh, no, I am with you guys 100 percent.' The next day, he defected."

Hilton didn't hold any resentment against Winter because "there were a lot of owners of other franchises in the AFL who would have preferred a franchise in the NFL."

Hilton felt more resentment against the NFL, particularly Bears owner George Halas, chairman of the older league's expansion committee. Halas had tried his best to sabotage the new league. He made a deal with Winter: pull out of the AFL at the last minute before the draft, and the NFL would reward him with a franchise.

"[Halas] wanted the college grads to get the feeling our league was falling apart and that they would be better off signing with the more established NFL," Hilton said.

On the very eve of the draft, the AFL was scrambling for a replacement team. At an emergency meeting, Hilton made a pitch for a team in Oakland.

"All you guys have rivalries except me," Hilton told the other owners. "You have to get me the opposition of a West Coast rivalry by putting a team in the Bay Area."

The problem was solved after a quick meeting with representatives of the hopeful Oakland team.

"We met at the San Francisco Hilton Airport hotel," Hilton said, remembering the meeting with Valley and a senator friend. "I made a pitch to them and that is how that franchise was put in Oakland."

Hunt's team in Dallas, Adams's in Houston, and Hilton's in Los Angeles were the "big three" of the AFL with virtually unlimited resources, more than even many teams in the NFL.

Those three teams were not only in good financial shape—they were lucky. They landed some of the best college talent available, outbidding the NFL for many star-quality players.

Hunt's Texans signed Abner Haynes, a running back from North Texas State who would lead the league in rushing and was the AFL's first Player of the Year and Rookie of the Year.

The Chargers signed Charlie Flowers, an all-American fullback from Mississippi, and Don Norton, a fleet, all-American receiver from Iowa, among many other great young players.

And the Oilers signed high-profile running back Billy Cannon from Louisiana State University along with other college all-Americans.

Not to mention some NFL players who turned out to be stars in the AFL, among them quarterback Jack Kemp, who was signed by the Chargers before his eventual trade to Buffalo, and Len Dawson, another outstanding quarterback who signed with the Dallas Texans after a brief fling with Pittsburgh and Cleveland.

It was not surprising that all three teams fared well on the gridiron in the early years of the AFL. The Oilers won league championships in 1960 and 1961, the Texans in 1962, and the Chargers (now

LEN DAWSON

Len Dawson was the epitome of cool when chaos was all around him. And there was plenty of chaos in the AFL, where shoot-outs were the norm and wild endings were surpassed only by wilder finishes the next week.

Yet Dawson never was shaken, not even when his name surfaced in connection to gamblers before Super Bowl IV. No, Dawson simply went out and did his job, performing so well that he made the Pro Football Hall of Fame in 1987.

Dawson was one of many players who started careers in the NFL before springing to stardom in the AFL.

"I was in Cleveland with the Browns when they started in 1960, and I remember Paul Brown saying don't pay any attention to that new league, it's operated by sons of rich people, it will never last a year," Dawson said. "And we were dumb enough to go with it, instead of thinking if it is successful, that's more jobs for players and coaches and support people."

Dawson had spent five years in the NFL—three with Pittsburgh and two with Cleveland—and didn't play much.

"I started maybe two games and never started and finished a game, other than holding for extra points and field goals," Dawson said.

"I asked Paul Brown for my release [in 1962] because they had drafted a quarterback, and I thought, after five years there is no way I am going to get an opportunity. He was kind enough to give it to me. He gave it to me in June, but some teams didn't know I was on the waiver wire because everyone was on vacation."

Hank Stram was paying attention, though. At the time, Stram was the coach of the AFL's Dallas Texans. He had been an assistant at Purdue and helped to recruit Dawson for the Boilermakers.

"Hank Stram mentioned if I ever get free, give him a call," Dawson said. "He contacted me when I cleared waivers; Buffalo also contacted me. Their general manager worked for Paul with the Browns, and whenever he put someone on waivers, the guy said to let him know and Paul did.

"Oakland was the other team that contacted me, but I knew Hank, and if I would ever get a good look, he would give it to me. He helped develop me at Purdue."

And he helped turn Dawson into one of the all-time greats.

Dawson was the AFL's player of the year in 1962, when he also led the league in passing and, by the way, took the Texans to the championship.

Dawson would lead the AFL in passing three more times and win two more AFL titles. Stram once called him "the perfect quarterback."

The perfect quarterback stayed cool under all kinds of trying circumstances, including a national scandal before the 1970 Super Bowl.

Dawson was one of several players named in connection with a federal gambling investigation. Thankfully, it faded away quickly. And Dawson's team was anything but distracted en route to a great Super Bowl victory.

Dawson completed only 12 passes for 142 yards, but his field generalship and his 46-yard scoring pass that clinched the 23–7 upset of heavily favored Minnesota earned him most valuable player honors.

That anyone considered it a shock was, well, stunning to Dawson and the Chiefs.

"I think we were the most talented AFL team ever," Dawson said. "We were a more veteran team. Most of the important guys were there for Super Bowl I and then for Super Bowl IV. Bobby Bell was in the first one, and he was gone, but we now had Willie Lanier and Jim Lynch and James Marsalis, who was a very important addition. But also we had the veteran people who had been there and who knew how to handle it better than the first time.

"We had Jan Stenerud, too; we didn't have him in Super Bowl I."

After the Chiefs had their Super Bowl victory, Dawson could have thumbed his nose at the league that didn't recognize his talent. He never did that.

"For us, it was feelings of relief that you have done it, it happened, all you worked for," he said.

It was a tough physical season for Dawson, who suffered a knee injury and was told by several orthopedists that he needed surgery.

There was one orthopedist, however, who recommended another course of action.

"He said to not put any weight on it for two weeks and see if it's just a strain, which worked in my favor," Dawson said. "Remember, they didn't have MRIs back then.

"I also spent five years in the NFL and didn't get to play, and now I was part of a world championship team. That was very satisfying. All I had wanted was the opportunity to see if I could perform."

Well, Len, you sure could.

based in San Diego) in 1963. The Texans, of course, would change addresses to Kansas City after the 1962 season and make appearances in two Super Bowls before the AFL and NFL officially completed their merger.

Other AFL franchises were not in the same class financially.

"There were some franchises that were trying to do it with mirrors and a shoestring," noted Chargers lineman Ron Mix, referring specifically to the New York Titans led by Wismer, the Denver Broncos spearheaded by Bob Howsam, and the Raiders featuring Valley. They weren't the only ones.

Nevertheless, all systems were "go" for the first season in 1960.

"Once we had eight teams, the number of teams necessary, we concentrated on the players," Hilton said. "We concentrated on the teams building themselves."

Hilton knew that it would take time to build a profit-making business—not only with his new football team but also with his credit-card business.

Both lost a lot of money at the start. His father couldn't help but notice.

"I have been looking at the financial results of Carte Blanche and the Chargers," Hilton's father said disapprovingly one day. "I noticed both of these lost a million dollars. What kind of record are you trying to set?"

Of course, things eventually got turned around in both businesses for Hilton, but not without a struggle—especially with the Los Angeles Chargers, who eventually moved to San Diego after one season in Los Angeles.

"I wasn't happy about [financial problems], but we felt we were going to be in the football business for a long period of time," Hilton recalled, "so it didn't discourage me. I think some of the other owners might have been more discouraged."

Chargers receiver Lance Alworth, one of the AFL's brightest stars, remembered Hilton as "a very personable man."

"He was a young guy at the time he owned the team," said Alworth, an all-American receiver from the University of Arkansas who was drafted by the Raiders in 1962 and traded to the Chargers.

"He was very available to the players and just had a smile on his face, a bubbly guy. I think he was happy most of the time because we were winning, and he was the reason why it happened."

Meanwhile, the people who ran teams in Denver, New York, and Oakland weren't always so happy.

Struggling with poor attendance, Howsam's Denver team was on the verge of folding at one point, the Titans were being sadly mismanaged by Wismer, and the Raiders were having front-office infighting among their many owners and problems gaining an identity in Oakland.

Remembered Patrick Sullivan, son of the Patriots' original owner, Billy Sullivan, "One little-known fact that is interesting: after the first year, the Titans were a mess. Harry Wismer was really struggling, and the Titans were on the verge of bankruptcy. Joe Foss, who was the commissioner of the league, put my father in charge of the Titans as well as the Patriots. My father effectively ran the Titans, at least from a financial standpoint, for the first half of the '61 season until it got stabilized, and then eventually the Phil Iselin–Leon Hess–Sonny Werblin group ended up buying them."

Meanwhile, there were rumors that Hunt himself was helping to finance some of the league's other teams just to keep the AFL afloat—a fact disputed by Hunt.

"The NFL people used to claim that I owned every team in the league," Hunt said.

However, Hunt did contribute his share when the AFL took over Wismer's failing New York franchise.

Wismer, a respected sports announcer, was a part owner of the Washington Redskins in the NFL before taking over the New York Titans in the AFL. It was an absolute necessity for the AFL to have

LARRY EISENHAUER

Eisenhauer, a defensive end for the Boston Patriots, was a four-time AFL all-star and named to the Patriots' 1960s all-decade team. A product of Boston College, Eisenhauer was known by his teammates as "The Wild Man" because of his emotional intensity. Following an early retirement, Eisenhauer opened his own business as a manufacturer's representative selling semiconductors.

I was always known as a guy that got himself very emotionally motivated before games. I was always able to get that adrenalin flowing and fired up. I had a reputation of just coming all the time, never stopping. The old-timers remember the "Wild Man."

I picked the AFL because I wanted to go where I had the best chance of making a team. And I felt it was with the Patriots because they only had two defensive ends, and one was going to be changed to a guard, so there was a slot there if I could make the team. That coupled with the Boston College connection were the reasons that I went there.

This was a new league, but I felt it was big time. It was just exciting to be a part of it. Only later on in life do you realize what a history-making part of sports that I happened to be part of. That meant a lot to me. And as I look back on my career, we always had a chip on our shoulders with the NFL because they always tried to downplay our talents in the early years, and I'm sure it was very valid. But it grew old as you got into the fourth and fifth season.

When they started playing exhibition games between the two leagues, we treated it like a Super Bowl, and we held our own with them.

When the Jets won the Super Bowl, I was so emotionally involved that there were tears in my eyes. I was so proud of what Joe Namath and the Jets had accomplished.

That was when it was out there and everyone could see that we could hold our own. We always believed in our hearts that we had a lot of players on each team that were every bit as good as some of the players at the same positions in the NFL. We didn't really say anything because that was the big mantra of the NFL, that we were inferior all the time. They would play that up. I remember particularly Tex Maule [of *Sports Illustrated*] and [Dallas Cowboys general manager] Tex Schramm used to do it all the time. It was downright insulting.

For a lot of right reasons, too, it was maybe true early on. But as we grew and survived, we got to be better. We got better players, better teams.

Things started to change. I saw more players that had credentials as all-Americans or all-conference players come into the American Football League, say after the third year, when it proved it was economically viable.

We had the Harry Wismer fiasco in New York, where some guys couldn't even cash their paychecks. So the league didn't show that it was going to be staying until it got a TV contract with ABC (and later with NBC). A lot of that money was used to grab these players that formerly wouldn't sign with the AFL, the big names.

So what I saw was a better quality of player coming into the league as the league got a little bit older. The players that came were more demanding, more difficult because you were playing against better players.

I knew when it was time for me to retire, even though I was only 29. I saw too many players hang on and really hurt themselves as they got older. And I had one knee injury. It wasn't bad, a torn cartilage. It didn't ruin my efficacy as far as pass rushing was concerned, but I felt it was time to move on.

I got a call from New Orleans, a dear friend who played with me, Eddie Khayat. He was from the Philadelphia Eagles and played his last couple of years with the Patriots. I believe he was a defensive coach [in New Orleans]. So he called me personally to offer a job. He offered me a two-year, no-cut contract at a 25 percent raise. I'll never forget him for that. It was over the top, and here I am not making a penny. But I decided at that point that that was it, and I called [Boston coach] Clive Rush back and said, "I'm formally retiring."

So I threw a party for myself at Gino Cappelletti's restaurant and bar called "The Point After" and invited Billy Sullivan and all the press. I think maybe 12 guys showed up. And I moved on, I closed the door, I felt it was time to go. Never looked back, ever. Never went to a Patriots practice, ever.

a franchise in New York. But Wismer had trouble filling the seats at the Polo Grounds. He had a habit of reporting overblown crowd figures to the media, making his franchise look more successful than it actually was.

Following a Titans game against the visiting Boston Patriots, sportswriter Red Smith wrote that Wismer announced that the game was witnessed by 25,000 fans. If that was the case, Smith said in so many words, 24,500 came disguised as empty seats, and the other 500 were Patriots owner Billy Sullivan's relatives.

Wismer was also slow in resolving debts.

"He didn't have the resources to really fight the NFL," Steadman recalled. "I can remember going up there [to New York] for a game. I'd have to go and try to get the money at the concessions at the end of the game to pay our airfare back."

Ron Hobson, who covered the Boston Patriots for the *Quincy (MA) Patriot-Ledger*, testified to the hard times in the early going of the AFL's New York team.

The Patriots were visiting New York, and Hobson, already in town for the 1962 World Series, went over to the Polo Grounds to gather material on the Boston football team. Hobson also did double duty as a spotter for Bob Murphy, the broadcaster for the Titans, as they were then known.

"It was my first time in the Polo Grounds," Hobson recalled. "I was a spotter in the scoreboard on the side of the second level. That's where the broadcast booth was. And you had to look out through the numbers, the holes where they place the inning numbers. We sat there and did that—Jesus Christ, what a rinky-dink place! Well, at halftime, the players had to walk up stairs to the locker rooms. They were in the end zone, actually in center field.

"And we're looking over there and we see both teams standing there in a line for like 10 minutes. Turns out the guy that supplied the oranges for Harry Wismer hadn't been paid. He had locked the locker room! They had to wait for the guy to get paid to open the door. They eventually got in."

Wismer eventually was replaced by the Iselin-Werblin-Hess group. But none could replace Wismer's charm and boyish sense of fun. He enjoyed the high life and especially enjoyed playing pranks on his fellow owners.

"Harry liked to have a couple of pops," Patrick Sullivan remembered. "He and my dad got to be pretty friendly."

It wasn't unusual for Wismer to call Sullivan's house in the early hours of the morning and play jokes on him. Once, he pretended to be Richard Cushing, the Cardinal of Boston, and another time President John F. Kennedy.

"My father knew President Kennedy—not well—but knew him enough that a phone call from him would not have been improbable," Patrick Sullivan said.

Wismer, the funnyman, was a kick to have around. Wismer, the businessman, didn't evoke too many smiles.

Of the teams that struggled most in the early going, Steadman said, "The worst one was the New York team. So the league took the team over at the end of the 1962 season."

The Raiders also had financial problems. And Valley, the optimistic owner who had coined the phrase "Foolish Club," was anything but optimistic after poor attendance at Raiders games in the first few years.

"It was just a lost cause," remembered Charlie Zeno, sports editor of the *Contra Costa Times*. "They were operating on a shoestring. Some guys panicked and bailed out."

Zeno said that the Raiders had trouble giving away tickets in the early days. He recalled that Scotty Stirling, the Raiders' public relations man, would stop by his office with free tickets. But hardly anyone wanted them.

"I'd have a dozen tickets, and if I could give away two, I felt successful," Zeno said.

The Patriots, meanwhile, were also having their money problems.

"The Patriots were underfinanced from the beginning," Steadman said. "We all marveled at how Billy Sullivan was able to hang in there. Many times, the other owners helped him out to keep him alive."

Sullivan and his wife had saved up $8,300 to buy a summer house on Cape Cod. When the opportunity to buy a football team came up, Sullivan was excited. "He talked my mother into buying the team," Patrick Sullivan said.

Of course, the $8,300 was not enough to buy the team alone. It was just a down payment of Sullivan's portion to meet the $250,000 franchise fee, according to his son.

There was more involved.

"Along with the franchise fee, my dad and his partners had to put up $500,000 in operating cash. They didn't want to put up that kind of money and couldn't put up the money, so they put up $100,000 and sold stock to raise the other $400,000. My father bought all that stock back in 1976."

What made Sullivan think the Patriots were going to make it?

"My father was the single most optimistic human being," Patrick Sullivan said. "He always believed that if you had a quality product, then people would come to it, and he had a basis to believe this."

Billy Sullivan had worked at Boston College when Frank Leahy was coaching there.

"He was publicity director dealing only with football. Boston College was the national champion, and they regularly played in front of large crowds at Fenway Park. My father saw with his own eyes that there was a following for football here."

That was the general thinking in other places as well when the upstart American Football League was launched in 1960 by Hunt.

Despite his great wealth, the hardworking Hunt was as down to earth as could be. Patrick Sullivan remembered when his dad came back once from a meeting with the 27-year-old Hunt, quite impressed.

"I remember my Dad coming back and saying he had just met Lamar Hunt, whose father at that point was the Bill Gates of the time, the wealthiest man in the world. My mother asked, 'What did you think of him?'

"My father said, 'He's a really nice young man. The problem is that he put his feet up on the desk, and he had holes in the bottom of his shoes.' But Lamar was fabulous. He was the most measured, most respectful [person], just an amazing guy. There are many true stories of instances where he would actually cast a vote that might have hurt his own team but knew it was better for the long-term benefit of the game."

Players remember Hunt as a beloved, respected figure.

"It was Lamar Hunt's team, and with Hank Stram as coach, it was a very professional operation," recalled Tommy Brooker, a place-kicker and end on the Texans. "Lamar was one of the guys, although you always knew he was the owner.

"He would come to practice and take off his coat and tie and put on a Texans T-shirt and would throw the ball to you. I started off as a third-team kicker. When I would kick in practice, he would toss the ball back to me. We always respected him. He was very polished and mild mannered. He had shown his support for us with his money, and he was pretty passionate about the team."

2

Cannon Fire

We competed for players, boy, did we! Yeah, everybody was
hiding players—the Chiefs had Buck Buchanan, and he was no
small fry, he was pretty difficult to hide.

—Cleveland Browns owner Art Modell

It was 1959, and the NFL had a
new competitor. No longer was the NFL the only league in town.

A signing war for players was on, and the AFL was going helmet
to helmet with the NFL.

Enter Billy Cannon.

For three years, he was a huge star at Louisiana State University
(LSU), a powerful halfback who led the Tigers to the national championship in the 1958 season.

The NFL corralled Cannon first, when the Los Angeles Rams
signed him as the number 1 pick in the draft.

So young Cannon was all smiles as he walked out of a Philadelphia
hotel room on a late fall day in 1959. He had just made a deal on a
three-year contract with the Rams that would net him a small fortune
of $50,000. He was a happy man. He had everything he wanted.

That was until the AFL stepped in.

Winner of the Heisman Trophy, the LSU halfback was important
to the AFL cause. A player of Cannon's stature would help legitimize

---

the new league. And the Oilers were ready to make him pro football's first $100,000 player.

The money, Cannon said, "was too great to resist."

The Oilers were owned by Texas oil millionaire Bud Adams and were one of the few teams in the AFL that could afford to spend that kind of money.

Billy signed with the AFL's Oilers. Now he had contracts with two teams in two different professional leagues.

The Rams filed suit to stop Cannon from playing with the Oilers.

So who was Billy Cannon, and why was he the center of a fierce tug-of-war?

Cannon grew up in North Baton Rouge, Louisiana, a rugged blue-collar neighborhood where his father worked as a janitor. At Istrouma High School, he starred in both football and track. He was tough and quick with his fists.

At LSU, he became an adored player—adored by Tigers fans and feared by opponents. One amazing runback of a punt marked the highlight of his college career and helped him in the Heisman Trophy voting.

It was 1959, a sultry Halloween night in LSU's Tiger Stadium. It was the stage for one of the biggest games in the South in many years. As defending national champion, LSU was ranked number 1. Hated Mississippi was number 6 in the battle of top 10 teams.

The Rebels sought revenge. The previous year, they had been victimized by the Tigers during LSU's run to the national title. This time, Rebels fullback Charlie Flowers made an unusual prediction.

Flowers promised to "outgain Billy Cannon," a remark that became prime bulletin-board material in the LSU locker room.

Everyone felt it would be a tight game. No one thought the defending national champions would lose the ball four times on fumbles and go three quarters without scoring a point.

But there it was, a 3–0 lead for Ole Miss on a field goal by Bob Khayat. Cannon, the classic campus hero, was suddenly the game's goat when his fumble set up the Mississippi field goal.

Early in the fourth quarter, the Rebels had third-and-17 on their 42 and decided to punt. Jake Gibbs, who later went on to a Major League Baseball career, kicked a skyscraper.

Still upset with his fumble that had helped Ole Miss take the lead, Cannon dropped back to his five-yard line to await Gibbs's kick.

The ball hit the turf and skidded inside the 20, taking a high bounce into Cannon's arms.

And he was off.

At the 19-yard line, Cannon shrugged off a blow to the knees from the Rebels' Richard Price, then slipped out of the grasp of Jerry Daniels, who had a clear shot at him. He carried the Mississippi tackler 10 yards before shedding him.

At the 40, Mickey Mangham threw a block that gave Cannon a little more running room. But by the time he had reached the 50, he was not yet in the clear.

Gibbs had a shot at the LSU star. Evading a block, he lunged at Cannon at the Mississippi 45—and missed.

Free sailing for Cannon the rest of the way.

"When I saw Johnny Robinson looking back for someone to block, I felt this was it," Cannon recalled later of his backfield mate. "Just don't stub your toe, I told myself."

He didn't, crossing the goal line for a touchdown that gave the Tigers a 7–3 victory.

Flowers, who had missed Cannon when the LSU star made a neat cut, paid him the ultimate compliment.

"It was like a high school player trying to tackle an all-American. He went through my hands like nothing."

Cannon's dramatic touchdown punt return, officially recorded at 89 yards, became part of LSU football lore and put the LSU–Ole Miss rivalry on a different level. No matter that the Tigers lost to the Rebels 21–0 and Cannon had a subpar game in a rematch at the Sugar Bowl—the LSU star was still the prince of college football.

He had won the Heisman Trophy as the nation's top collegiate football player by a 3–1 margin over his closest competitor, Penn State's Richie Lucas. The 89-yard punt return weighed heavily in the Heisman voting, Larry Grantham recalled.

"At Mississippi, we scored 337 points and gave up 21 in 11 ball games and we beat LSU in the Sugar Bowl," said Grantham, who starred for the New York Jets. "But everyone remembered Billy Cannon for that long run he had against us during the season. I used to run into him during the [AFL] days and say, 'You need to buy me shoes for my babies, you got the Heisman Trophy because of me.'"

And Cannon also had a rich pro contract in his pocket, thanks to the NFL's Rams.

Then he had two.

The Rams sought a court injunction to prevent Cannon from playing with the Oilers. Pete Rozelle, the Rams' general manager who had signed Cannon and later became the NFL commissioner, was ferociously single-minded.

"The Rams intend to enforce the contract," he said.

This legal entanglement was one of many battles between the NFL and AFL as the new league attempted to establish itself with the signing of top college talent.

LSU's star halfback was only one of 425 players taken in the first AFL player draft in December 1959, but clearly his was the most compelling story.

In a time of double signings, double-dealing, and litigation, Cannon was in the middle of a battle between two professional leagues. It was all part of the standard operating procedure as both the AFL and NFL went after the nation's fresh college talent to fortify their rosters.

The battle was on.

"There were lots of shenanigans going on," said Jon Morris, a six-time AFL all-star with the Boston Patriots. "They were signing players before the draft. They were giving money to agents. As an offensive lineman, I wasn't part of that. But I heard some stories."

One story was about Joe Don Looney, an Oklahoma fullback who played with Morris on the Senior Bowl team:

"One time about five of us were sitting around the bar talking about which teams we signed with," Morris recalled. "And Looney says, 'You guys are nuts. I was drafted by the Giants and by Kansas City and I signed with both of them.'"

Why?

"Looney said, 'Well, because they both offered money. I got bonuses from both of them and I cashed both their checks.' I said, 'There's a good way to do it. Why didn't I think of that?'"

Along with the players' double signings, there was also subterfuge aplenty—devious tricks that matched a Hollywood spy thriller.

The AFL and NFL went to great extremes to sign players by using the common so-called practice of babysitting. Team officials would actually hide players in hotels and elsewhere so that the other league couldn't find them.

Al Locasale, a longtime key figure in the management of three teams, the San Diego Chargers, Oakland Raiders, and Cincinnati

BILLY SHAW

The Buffalo Bills' guard is the only player in the Pro Football Hall of Fame who played his entire career in the AFL. Shaw played in 119 games for the Bills from 1961 to 1969 and was an all-star selection for eight straight years. He played on AFL title–winning teams in 1964 and 1965. Following retirement from football, Shaw moved to Toccoa, Georgia, and opened a concrete business.

The Bills were a perfect fit for me. We didn't throw the ball as much as the other teams. We were a running team with a lot of wide sweeps and traps. Georgia Tech was basically the same way, and Marvin Bass was my line coach in college, and he became my line coach at Buffalo. So all the cards kind of fell right for me because the system wasn't a lot different.

[In the AFL], I played a different position. I was a tackle in college. But we did a lot of tackle pulls and that kind of stuff at Georgia Tech. So foot speed was my plus because we ran the football featuring the guard getting out in front.

The Bills told me they wanted to play me on either the defensive side of the ball or offensive side, as defensive end or offensive guard. And the [Dallas] Cowboys ended up drafting me and in preliminary talks wanted to draft me as a linebacker, and I didn't want to make a position move going into the pros.

So I went to my college coach, who was Bobby Dodd, a legend. He told me there is a place in sports for a second league. He said I'd probably have an opportunity to play quicker [with the Bills] because I wouldn't be learning a new position. And he said I would be part of sports history by choosing the Bills over the Cowboys.

I loved playing in Buffalo. They call Buffalo a small market. As a player, I never saw that.

The people were so appreciative of what we accomplished. They were so appreciative that the team was there, I just didn't even think about playing in a so-called major market like Dallas or New York. I couldn't have cared less about that. I really enjoyed my nine seasons in Buffalo, and I really enjoyed the people. My wife and I to this day have lasting friendships with the fans that go back to the sixties. We've grown old together.

People talk about the great battles I had with Ernie Ladd. That goes back to the college all-stars, the game that was played in Chicago. I was playing defensive tackle, and I was playing behind Ernie, Bob Lilly, and Houston Antwine, who became one of the premier tackles in the AFL. When you talk about tackles in the AFL, you talk about Houston Antwine, and then you talk about Ernie Ladd and then Buck Buchanan.

At this particular all-star game, I was playing defensive tackle, and Houston Antwine was playing offensive guard. And I was stinking it up pretty bad, but not nearly as bad as Houston Antwine was stinking it up at offensive guard. Otto Graham, the coach, swapped us. He moved me to offensive guard and Houston to defensive tackle. And so for the rest of that practice session, I'm going one-on-one with Houston Antwine, Ernie Ladd, and Bob Lilly. Fortunately for me, Bob was playing for Dallas [in the NFL]. But I still had Ernie Ladd, Buck Buchanan, and Houston Antwine to deal with [in his career]. And they're beating the hell out of me (in the college all-stars practice). It just so happened that Buck Buchanan and Ernie Ladd were the two biggest players in football in the day. (Ladd was 6-foot-9 and 315 pounds and Buchanan 6-7, 270.)

I was 6-2 and 252 at the time, so I'm giving away a whole bunch of height and a whole bunch of weight. We had some tremendous battles against one another. Fortunately, I got a tip that helped me in these battles. When Ernie got into his three-point stance, he would cock his arm, the one he was going to bring up with a forearm. He would bring it back ever so slightly, and that would give you time to get set. One of the coaches at the all-star game noticed it and told me about it. I never told a soul . . . never told Ernie Ladd because if he corrected that, he'd be knocking my head off.

Bengals, recalled, "We took Harry Schuh, a big tackle out of Memphis State, and Al [Davis] hid him in Hawaii. The kid was asked where he wanted to go, and he said Hawaii. The Hiltons, having all those hotels, were involved in trying to help all the AFL teams and they got us rooms for the players.

"There was a kid from Nebraska I was trying to sign, and we could get these kids the biggest suite in a hotel, and when their parents came in to visit, they were staying in the presidential suite, and the manager of the hotel was running around serving them. That created an aura that was helpful, and word got around among the players."

Another babysitter story, as told by longtime NFL executive Joe Browne:

"After the first common draft, one of Pete Rozelle's friends, Jack Landry, a marketing guy for Marlboro who was one of the 'babysitters,' came up to the stage. It was about 5:30 p.m., and Jack walked up to Pete on the podium and asked him, 'Pete, I got three Michigan State linebackers in a motel in Yonkers, what am I supposed to do?' Everybody cracked up."

Davis, who served on the Chargers' coaching staff in Los Angeles with Sid Gillman early in his career, was responsible for bringing a lot of the top college talent to the AFL. This included Lance Alworth, the Chargers' all-time great receiver known as "Bambi" for his quickness and graceful deerlike strides.

"Al spent a lot of time getting very close to Alworth's attorney, a guy named Starr," Locasale said.

Davis also got to know the people who ended up being decision makers: girlfriends, wives, and friends. They helped players choose the AFL.

Locasale, meanwhile, kept an eye on the players.

"I would find out what hotel an [NFL] team was staying in and would get a room there, and then meet with the players, listen to the conversations with the players.

"At one place, the GM of a team sees me in the lobby and says, 'You can't be here, you are in a rival league.' And I said, 'I have a room, this is a public area, I am allowed to be here and this is where I'm staying.' The hotel manager says, 'He can be in any public area of the hotel. I can't throw him out.'"

Hotels weren't the only place where players were stashed. Lamar Hunt, whose Dallas Texans were the flagship team of the new league, had his own plane. There he had players flying high, literally and figuratively.

"The Chiefs had the use of the Hunt's airplane and would sign kids in the airplane," Locasale remembered. "I was on the private plane flying over a ranch somewhere in Texas with some players, and they were talking about food, and Lamar points down to the ground and says, 'See those cattle down there, pick one out, that is where your steak will come from.'"

The AFL was successful in signing many top prospects for other reasons as well.

"In the early '60s, players with the NFL would stay with the teams all of the time," remembered Larry Eisenhauer, who chose the AFL over the NFL with the Boston Patriots. "There were very few trades, certainly no free agency, nothing like that. You had guys that would be playing together for five, six years, and it was hard for a rookie to break in, unless he was a superstar."

The AFL featured more opportunity for new players, especially those just starting out in pro ball. At the AFL draft, Hunt said the league would have 264 job openings, while the NFL would only have about 20 openings.

Said Don Rossi, administrative director of the Dallas Texans, "We'll put it to the kids that way, and it becomes a matter of simple arithmetic to see which way they'll go."

The first year of the league, 1960, four of five players who made the college all-America backfield signed with AFL teams: Cannon with Houston, halfback Ron Burton of Northwestern with Boston, fullback Flowers with the Los Angeles Chargers, and quarterback Lucas with Buffalo.

The all-America team also listed Army halfback Bob Anderson, who later played one NFL season with the New York Giants.

"[Signings of the all-Americans] meant that immediately there were players of name quality coming from college into this new league, so you didn't have to depend on guys who were retreads from the NFL," Locasale said. "You were getting guys who had a reputation for being outstanding players when coming out of the college ranks. And many of them were outstanding in the AFL."

Some of the other players, like Cannon, signed with both leagues. Then the NFL went into its prevent defense with a number of lawsuits against the AFL. Cannon was the focal point in the most highly celebrated of these cases.

Even though AFL commissioner Joe Foss had promised not to get into a money war with the NFL over players, that's exactly what happened.

Foss, the former governor of South Dakota and a World War II flying hero with the marines, was hired as commissioner just two days before the AFL draft. He planned to set up league headquarters in Dallas, home of Hunt's Texans.

"Foss was the league's unanimous choice," Hunt said, adding that the league had considered 25 men and interviewed eight.

If the AFL owners wanted someone with steel nerves and an iron hand to run their league, then Foss was their man. During World II, Foss won the Congressional Medal of Honor for his numerous aerial battles with the Japanese. In one four-month period, Foss blasted 26 Japanese planes out of the sky.

As a college student, Foss had played football—barely. It wasn't until his last game as a senior at South Dakota that he won a starting job at guard.

He eventually found politics to be a game more to his liking. He served two terms in the South Dakota legislature before becoming governor in 1954. He won the race for governor again in 1956, but South Dakota's two-term law kept Foss from immediately going after a third term.

At the age of 44, he became the AFL commissioner. The league owners offered Foss an "open-end" contract, but he wanted to sign on for only a three-year period. The job paid him "around $30,000" per year, Foss said.

Actually, Foss didn't see a salary for a while.

"I worked the first six weeks for nothing," he told *Sports Illustrated*, "because the league had no money. I started traveling around the country. Some of the owners criticized me for not spending enough time in league cities, but I realized that people in the small towns had television sets, and we had to have ratings or we could get no sponsors and no big television contracts."

Foss hoped to arrange a meeting with NFL officials to set up "some type of salary agreement" so that the leagues would not go broke trying to outbid each other.

"We have no intention of trying to outbuy the NFL," Foss said. "For our part, we'll be more than happy to keep salaries as they are now in professional football. Naturally, though, there'll be some bidding for top stars. We understand that, and we're equipped."

The league that Foss took over was pretty much nothing more than franchises on paper for proposed teams in Dallas, New York, Minneapolis–St. Paul, Denver, Houston, Buffalo, Los Angeles, and Boston. Minneapolis–St. Paul eventually dropped out to join the NFL and was replaced by Oakland.

RON MIX

*Ron Mix was one of the top offensive tackles in the AFL, helping the
San Diego Chargers win the league title in 1963. A graduate of the
University of Southern California, Mix had the distinction as one of
only 20 men who played in the entire 10 years of the AFL. He was
an AFL all-star nine of those years.*

*Another distinction: in 11 professional seasons, he was called for
only two holding penalties, and he says they were both "bad calls."
During the off-season, Mix earned a law degree and became an attorney in California following his retirement from football.*

I was the number 1 draft choice of the Baltimore Colts, who
were the world champions. I wanted to play for them. I was
also drafted by the Boston Patriots of the AFL, and I was contacted by the Patriots and told them that if I had to go back
East, it would definitely be with the NFL.

Then they called me back and said they were cooperating
with other teams in the league because they wanted to sign
the top players. "If we traded your rights to the Los Angeles
Chargers, would you consider playing for them?" I said, yes.
So that's what they did, and then the Baltimore Colts offered
me what was the going rate at that time, a $1,000 bonus and a
$7,500 salary. The Chargers offered me two years guaranteed at
$12,000 a year, plus a $5,000 bonus.

A huge difference, but I wanted to play for the Colts. So I
contacted Weeb Ewbank and told him about the offer from
the Chargers. I said I'd still rather play for the Colts. If they
gave me a $2,000 bonus and a $10,000 one-year contract, I
would sign with them. He said, "Ron, that's like Johnny Unitas money. That would disrupt our whole salary structure."
Ewbank didn't think the AFL was going to last more than one
year, anyway. So he said, "Sign with the Chargers, and we'll
see you next year."

Well, next year came, and the AFL was still hanging in
there. There were some franchises in the AFL that were trying to do it with mirrors and a shoestring. And that would be
Oakland, New York, and Denver. The other teams were pretty

well funded with people of individual wealth greater than the NFL teams.

But that wasn't the only reason the AFL made it. The AFL made it because the NFL did not take them seriously, did not think they would last. So they allowed about 70 percent of the best players in the first four years to go to the new league. They didn't want to compete with them financially. And they didn't begin to take the league seriously until Joe Namath signed . . . a well publicized four-year contract of unheard-of money for the time, $100,000 a year.

The AFL game was starting to catch on to the public's fancy because they brought in a lot of innovative coaches like Hank Stram and Sid Gillman and Al Davis. It was a great product.

What was great from my perspective was that I was very fast for an offensive lineman, and so Sid Gillman designed some plays that were kind of unique . . . tackle-pull plays. Usually an offensive lineman labors in the middle where nobody sees him, but I got to pull out and lead [Keith] Lincoln and [Paul] Lowe on sweeps. It brought me some attention.

We had great offensive players on the team, and so historically, it's been forgotten about our defense, but the defense was outstanding. Picture this, in the early sixties, a defensive line featuring Ernie Ladd, 6-9, 340; Earl Faison, 6-5, 285; Dick Hutson I think was 6-5, 280 . . . I mean, we were big on defense.

You take two of those players, Ernie Ladd and Earl Faison, before injuries cut them down, each of them played their position as well as anybody *ever* played . . . not just that they played their positions well but played them as well as anybody ever played.

I didn't miss a game until my tenth year when I had a knee sprain and missed six weeks. There was a reason I stayed free of injuries—I worked out, year-round.

It was a huge advantage. Gigantic advantage. I could lift 325 pounds above my head. What confidence that is when you know the guy you're playing against is 250, 260, but you could lift him over your head if you needed to.

First assignment for the new clubs: hire coaches.

The biggest name among them was "Slingin'" Sammy Baugh, who took on the coaching job with the New York Titans. Considered one of the greatest players in pro football history, the Hall of Fame quarterback opened up the passing game with his rocket arm in Washington and set records that stood for decades.

Sid Gillman, a refugee from the NFL where he coached the Los Angeles Rams for five years, signed on with the Los Angeles Chargers.

Eddie Erdelatz had a strong eight-year stint with the Naval Academy before signing to coach the Oakland Raiders.

Other coaching signings: Lou Saban with Boston, Frank Filchock with Denver, Hank Stram with Dallas, Buster Ramsey with Buffalo, and Lou Rymkus with Houston.

At the time of Foss's signing as commissioner on November 30, 1959, the AFL had no announced players, although some had already been singled out privately as draft picks.

One of these was Cannon, who made his intention known loud and clear at the NFL draft on November 30. "Cannon appeared at the meeting and said he would sign with the Rams after LSU's game with Mississippi in the Sugar Bowl Jan. 1," the Associated Press reported.

That was before Cannon was blown away by the offer from the Houston Oilers—more than twice the amount offered by the Rams.

Following LSU's loss to Ole Miss in the Sugar Bowl, Cannon signed a contract with the Oilers. Cannon was standing under the goalposts of the Sugar Bowl field when he signed the richest contract in pro football. Making note of Cannon's poor performance that day, one sportswriter cracked that when the halfback signed with the Oilers on the field, it was the only time all day that he had reached the end zone.

The reported contract: a $20,000 signing bonus and $30,000 per year for three seasons for a total deal of $110,000. That wasn't all, according to some reports.

The Oilers threw a new car into the deal, reported one source. The team set up a string of "Billy Cannon Health Centers" in Texas with Billy the nominal head, according to another report. There were also reports that Adams would cut Cannon in on profits from his service stations.

While Cannon agreed to a deal with the Oilers, backfield mate Johnny Robinson signed with the Texans. Like Cannon, LSU's number 2 halfback signed on the Sugar Bowl turf following the game as a symbolic gesture.

Hunt's Dallas team also picked up two other top-flight running backs: Jack Spikes of Texas Christian University and Abner Haynes of North Texas State. The Haynes signing was particularly significant because he was among the early crop of players mined by the AFL in the smaller historically black schools.

While Cannon created a firestorm with his double signing, a high-level meeting took place involving Foss and Rozelle, who had taken over as NFL commissioner following the premature death of Bert Bell.

The two commissioners met for four hours and reached a "no-raiding" agreement, among other things. The commissioners agreed not to tamper with players in the other league.

Little mention was made of Cannon's situation, although Rozelle said, "We talked about double contract signings. Foss told me he has not had an opportunity to investigate the double signings but would look into it."

The truce didn't last long. Within a week, the New York Giants claimed that one of their former scouts was paid $1,000 by the AFL's Los Angeles Chargers to sign players already under contract to the NFL club. The Giants accused Ed McKeever, who had become general manager of the Boston Patriots, and the Chargers of "fraud, deceit, bribery, and double-dealing."

Meanwhile, Cannon was embroiled in a bitter, higher-profile contract battle of his own with one of the NFL's teams.

Among numerous lawsuits, the Cannon case was the most eagerly anticipated.

Finally, on June 20, 1960, a decision came down. Blared a *New York Times* headline, "Judge Rules Pact with Club Invalid."

The court ruled that the Rams' signing of Cannon was illegal because he had yet to finish his college career.

A subheadline read, "Cannon Now Is Free to Play with Oilers in New Loop."

AFL 1, NFL 0.

The decision by a federal judge in Los Angeles gave the AFL its biggest victory in the player war with the NFL.

In the first year of the AFL, the Oilers lost $710,000, according to Adams—$70,000 to settle the Cannon case.

Adams couldn't complain about Cannon's value—at least in the early years of his pro career.

Cannon led the Oilers to three division crowns and two AFL titles. (In 1960, he scored on an 88-yard pass play to help Houston win the AFL title with a 24–16 victory over the Chargers. In 1961, the Chargers had moved to San Diego, but the title game wound up with the same result, Cannon scoring the only touchdown on a pass play as the Oilers clinched their second straight championship, 10–3.)

In 1961, Cannon put together an amazing season with 2,043 all-purpose yards. That year, he led the AFL in rushing.

In one game against the Titans in 1961, Cannon scored five touchdowns, a standard shared by only three players in AFL history.

Although Cannon was hampered by a back injury, he went on to a solid, if not spectacular, pro career. Traded to the Oakland Raiders in 1964, Cannon was converted from a running back into a tight end by coach Al Davis. He was a strong blocker and sure-handed receiver, scoring 10 touchdowns in 1967, and made all-league that season.

In the 1967 season, Cannon helped the Raiders gain a place in the Super Bowl, which they lost to Green Bay.

By the time he retired in 1970 after 11 years in the pros, Cannon was already on his way to a new career: dentistry. He had earned his degree while still playing football. In a matter of time, he was earning a reported $300,000 a year from his thriving dental practice in Baton Rouge.

Then, shocking news: In the summer of 1983, Cannon was arrested and charged with participating in a $6 million counterfeiting scheme. Cannon, known for a quick wit, still found something humorous in the situation.

"I did a bad thing," Cannon said. "I don't think it was so bad, but the Secret Service really got offended."

Cannon was sentenced to a five-year prison term but was released after serving about half of it.

"He was an all-American, all-world, and he let it slip away," Don Purvis, a teammate of Cannon's at LSU, told the *New York Times*. "That kind of tarnish is difficult to overcome."

Yes, but not enough to keep Cannon from restoring some brilliance.

Cannon's dental practice had turned sour. Looking for work, he was hired at the dental clinic at the state penitentiary in Angola, Louisiana. There, he helped the warden overhaul the clinic and provide good dental care for prisoners and jobs for other dentists.

The most popular sports figure in Louisiana history had, at least in one way, found a path to redemption as memorable as any of his long-distance runs.

3

Stadium Stories

There were no fans in the stands, which was no surprise
because we were playing in the Polo Grounds.

—Larry Grantham, original member
of the New York Titans

Cold showers and hot fans. Ah,
the delights of playing football in the "Rockpile."

War Memorial Stadium in Buffalo, New York, the so-called Rockpile, was originally built in the 1930s as part of President Franklin
Roosevelt's Works Progress Administration program.

"The War Memorial was nasty," says Hall of Fame quarterback
Len Dawson, reflecting on one of his least favorite AFL stadiums in
the 1960s.

Whenever his Kansas City Chiefs played in the Bills' notorious stadium, there would always be some kind of interaction with the fans.

Trouble happened when the announcer started introducing the
starting lineups. The tunnels leading to the field were dangerously
close to the fans.

"If they introduced the offense, you never walked onto the field during the intros because it was too dangerous," Dawson said. "You would
wonder, what would they throw at you? They threw stuff at their own
players, so you knew they were going to throw stuff at you."

Before facing the fans, visiting players at the Rockpile had to deal with another bothersome issue.

"If you were waiting, right before you went out to the field, there was a coffee urn. I don't think they ever cleaned it in all the years we went there," Dawson said with a chuckle.

As the team stood there, a noxious odor emanating from the urn filled the air.

"It smelled awful enough to make you sick before you even got on the field," Dawson said.

As the AFL went into its hurry-up offense in the early 1960s to find homes for its games, every player found something to hate or love about the odd assortment of stadiums in the league. Each had its own unique personality, for better or worse. Mostly for worse.

Teams scrambled around playing anywhere they could—inadequate high school fields, college stadiums, even creaky, old baseball parks badly in need of repair.

"Stadiums back in those days were pretty bad," Dawson said.

Just walking off the War Memorial field to the locker rooms could be a real adventure.

"You had to walk up a ramp where trucks would make deliveries, and you did that just to get to the stairs," Dawson said. "Then you had to walk up a couple flights to get to the locker room. I wouldn't call it a locker room, not by today's standards. It had maybe two commodes and a couple of showerheads might work."

Players weren't always lucky enough to get a hot shower.

The Bills may not have been too hospitable. But, in truth, the locker room was no better for them than for visiting players.

George Saimes, a Bills safety, recalled, "We didn't have enough chairs to go around. Guys would sit on milk cartons sometimes when we ran out of chairs doing our game plan."

Once the players reached the field, there were always surprises in store, as Dawson recalled.

"We played the championship game there in 1966, and that field had three different conditions: in some spots, not too bad. Or other spots where the sun never got to the field and it was frozen. Or one part was very sloppy where the sun hit the field.

"Remember, they didn't spend money on locker rooms and fields back in those days."

Or lights.

"The lights weren't the best," said Ed Rutkowski, who played a number of positions for the Bills from 1963 to 1968. "I used to return punts. I think it was Jerrel Wilson from the Kansas City Chiefs, he would punt the ball so high, it would go above the lights. So you'd see the ball, and then you wouldn't see it, and then you'd see it coming back down."

War Memorial was in a tough neighborhood. "One afternoon we came out after a game, and we're waiting by the buses to go to the airport," recalled Gil Santos, longtime broadcaster for the Patriots. "There was a bunch of us, broadcasters, newspaper guys, and players and coaches, and we're all talking, shooting the breeze, waiting to get on the buses.

"All of a sudden, here comes three police cars zooming up the street, and they stop in front of a house which is right where we were standing next to the buses. We're watching this, and the police go charging up the stairs. A couple of shots ring out from inside the house. Well, we tear around to the other side of the bus, and we're hiding as these shots are being fired. We hear a big commotion, and we look around the buses, and here come the police, hauling this guy out. I'll never forget it: he had handcuffs on behind his back, and the police are dragging him out by his feet. And there were three or four steps leading down to the sidewalk, and I remember his head bouncing off each step as he's going down the steps. I said to myself, holy smoke, what kind of a place is this? It was a scary moment."

Broadcasting a game at War Memorial could be a challenging experience. Remembered Santos, "It was difficult to broadcast a game from there because the stadium was built with girders, and you had to keep looking around the girders to see where the ball was and where the players were."

The addition of an upper deck and a roof made the game visually challenging for some fans.

"If you tried to sit underneath the roof, then you were going to be behind a pole," remembered Billy Shaw, an eight-time all-star guard for the Bills. "There were poles everywhere. It was kind of a difficult stadium in which to watch a game."

He knew because complaints were rampant from the players' wives who were stuck behind poles and couldn't see.

Despite everything, War Memorial did have some advantages for the home team.

ED ABRAMOSKI

Ed Abramoski was the Bills' trainer for 37 years starting from the first game in 1960. He was the first trainer on the team to be honored with a plaque in the Wall of Fame at Ralph Wilson Stadium.

I grew up in Erie, Pennsylvania. My dad worked in a steel mill. I was a head trainer at the University of Detroit and a gameday trainer for the Detroit Lions when I was offered the job of trainer with the Bills. I started in 1960, first game.

All of my family was either Browns or Steelers fans, and they told me the American Football League wouldn't last. I felt, hey, if the league folds, I have a résumé that I was with a pro team. I was a young guy at the time, 24, 25 . . . so I took the job. It kept me close to home, and here I got 37 years out of it.

I really enjoyed my job. I didn't think it was a lot of work. I remember I was the only trainer. I had one high school coach, and we'd tape a hundred guys before the practices. In those days, the guys didn't come in to camp in shape, so the training camp was eight weeks. There would be three, four weeks of scrimmaging and all that stuff. It would last forever. The guys wouldn't be in shape, and they'd get 'em in shape.

The guys loved the game. They were playing for peanuts. I remember when guys were holding out for $500 and they wouldn't get it. Most of the guys worked in the off-season. Some were only making $7,000, $8,000 in the game in the sixties.

The guys were all terrific guys. I keep in contact with most of them. I had a lot of fun with Al Beemiller, Stu Barber, George Saimes, Billy Shaw . . . Billy asked me to be his presenter when he went into the Hall of Fame. I was the first trainer to be a presenter for a player going to the Hall, and Billy was the first player [to go into the Hall] to play his whole career in the American Football League.

The league made the football pointier so you could throw it better. They used to call us a "basketball league in cleats" because we had 40–30 games. The owners in those days wanted to score points, so the people would come out. They wouldn't want to see a 3–0 game. They'd like to see a 40–30 game where

George Blanda would throw 60 passes. At the time, I remember the guys in *Sports Illustrated* were against the league. They didn't think the league had a chance.

In the off-season, I did some scouting. I scouted in all the territories that nobody else wanted—Wyoming and North Dakota and South Dakota, Utah, that was my territory. We got some good players like Spain Musgrove and Jim Lemoyne from Utah.

Every time I go up to the stadium, I see my name [on the Wall of Fame]. It's something else, to be recognized as one of the best. It's a great honor—a kid from a little town in Pennsylvania, a blue-collar town.

"It was basically a baseball stadium converted to a football field," Rutkowski said. "You got down on one end zone, and you were on a dirt infield. I played my last year as the Bills' quarterback, and I always said I couldn't play on artificial turf because there would be no places to draw plays in the dirt."

Rutkowski recalled that Bills quarterback Jack Kemp would do exactly that, showing what kind of a pattern a wide receiver should run.

"And they always had the pitcher's mound. They never really leveled it off. They had it on a rise from a quarter foot to almost a half foot."

That provided an edge for the Bills, according to Rutkowski.

"We used a certain pattern down there because if you were a defensive back and you were backpedaling and you hit that pitcher's mound, 9 times out of 10 you'd fall down.

"We knew if we got the defensive back going in the right direction backwards, he'd stumble most of the time. It was literally a home-field advantage."

It was also advantageous for the Bills to have the comfort of playing in familiar surroundings on a week-to-week basis. In the early days of the AFL, many teams were forced to play in a number of different stadiums.

The Patriots, for instance, played home games at Boston College, Boston University, Harvard University, and Fenway Park. Once the Pats even played a "home" game in Birmingham, Alabama, because Fenway was being used by the Red Sox for the World Series.

"Before the season, the players sometimes didn't know where they would be playing their home games," Len Dawson said of the Patriots.

If it was Fenway, it represented a real challenge to the broadcasting crew—sometimes a hazardous challenge.

"Many of these stadiums were not really made to broadcast pro football games," Santos said. "When we had a game at Fenway, we didn't have a broadcast booth as such. They put a wooden shack, maybe 12 by 12 feet, up on the roof, down the right-field line and put us at midfield.

"There were a couple of problems—one being that you had no bathroom facilities. You had to go down into the stands. Oh, it was tough. At halftime, you had to scramble down and get to the fan level to use the bathrooms, then get back upstairs in time to go on for the second half. We cut it pretty close many times. That was one problem. The other problem was that there was no heat in there. In the winter, it was cold as hell. And it was windy. If it was a windy day, that booth would shake, rattle, and roll. There were times we'd think, 'Oh, my God, this thing is going to blow over, and we're going to go flying off the edge, with no place to go.' Fortunately, it never happened."

When it was windy, Santos found the conditions "brutal."

"The wind would come off the Charles River, and that would be pretty cold."

It wasn't state of the art, but Santos noted, "You could see everything from our location to broadcast."

Well, almost everything. There was one instance when the Patriots were leading late in the game, and the visiting team was driving for a score.

"It was either Houston or Kansas City," Santos said. "They threw a pass in the end zone, and it was broken up. It wasn't until we saw films later that a fan wearing a trench coat had jumped down from the right-field seats, and he ran through the end zone and knocked the pass down, and nobody saw it."

For Jon Morris, center on the Patriots' all-decade team of the 1960s, playing in Fenway Park was the "most fun I had playing football in my entire life.

"The games were played on Friday nights. The place was filled—35,000 to 40,000 people there on a Friday night. The AFL didn't want to compete with the NFL on Sunday. And Fenway had an electric atmosphere. We were winning in the early days, and Fenway

GIL SANTOS: LONGTIME PLAY-BY-PLAY BROADCASTER FOR THE PATRIOTS

I was working at a media market station in New Bedford, Massachusetts, doing a DJ show and high school football and basketball games and saw in the Boston paper that the Patriots had changed flagship stations, going to WBZ. So I sent WBZ an air check of a high school football and high school basketball game I had done. They brought me up for an interview and hired me. That was pretty much it, cut and dry.

I was only 24 years old. I was a young kid. It was very, very exciting, to go on the air with a powerhouse like WBZ, be a voice of the Patriots at that time.

It was 1966. The players and the coaches in the American Football League felt the people in the NFL looked down on the AFL. Then the Jets beat the Colts, and that was a very, very, very huge turn of events for the AFL.

There was an article written in the local paper in New Bedford. The sports editor was a friend of mine. He called me to ask me prior to the game what I thought was going to happen. I said, I think the Jets can win the game. I said I think they can run it, and I think they can throw it against Baltimore. I think Baltimore's weakness is their defensive secondary, and I think Namath can carve 'em up. And of course he did. And that was step number 1, and then step number 2 came the next year when Kansas City did the same thing to Minnesota.

Now we get to the merger, and everybody's in the National Football League to live happily ever after. But leading up to it there was animosity among the players and coaches and people in the AFL, broadcasters, writers, all of us. We felt they were looking down their noses at us, and it was very, very exciting to see the AFL win those two Super Bowls just prior to the 1970 merger.

Boston was not a football town, and Billy Sullivan, bless his heart, took a chance. He did not have the capital like the Hunt family did in Kansas City and several of the other AFL owners. But he kept the team afloat, and they were pretty good.

He was a very nice man to work for. The-glass-was-always-half-full kind of guy. He always thought things were going to work out.

He was very much intent on keeping the team in New England, and even when things started to get rough, he kept it afloat, scratching and clawing as best he could for as many years as they needed to gain a foothold for fans.

The Patriots had a small group of hard-core fans. They had the 1776 Club, which was comprised of the season-ticket holders. They drew some pretty good crowds when they played in Fenway Park against good teams like Buffalo and Kansas City, the Oakland Raiders, and the Jets. And they were more than competitive. But it was a struggle [to draw support generally] because for many years the only pro football that New England people had seen was Giants football. So there was a really strong Giants fan base in New England.

That was another struggle, trying to convince the Giants fans that, hey, take a look at our team, give us a chance to show you what we can do. So that was another early AFL struggle for the Patriots. They didn't know if they could convert the Giants fans, but they wanted them to at least watch us so that *their* children would become Patriots fans. That's pretty much what happened over the course of time.

Park came alive on Friday nights. Even today, I talk to people who live in the Boston area who remember the Friday nights at Fenway Park and how much fun it was."

Fenway's most identifiable feature is the "Green Monster"—the fabled left-field wall at the Red Sox ballpark. For football games, fans would sit in temporary bleachers set up in front of the legendary wall.

Can you identify this? Morris will ask friends, pointing to an old photo.

"I have a picture of me playing with the Patriots," he said. "We're running a draw play. Babe Parilli has just handed Jim Nance the ball. And in the background, you could see the Red Sox bullpen. I show people this picture, and when I tell them it's Fenway Park, they can't believe it."

Among the other eastern teams, the New York Titans had the distinction of playing in another famous ballpark—the Polo Grounds.

The old New York Giants' stadium was the site of many famous baseball moments, including a legendary catch by Willie Mays in the 1954 World Series.

"I was a big baseball fan as a kid, and to be able to stand where Willie Mays made that catch in center field was a big thrill," said Larry Grantham, a linebacker with the original New York Titans before they became the Jets. "Walking on that field was kind of sacred."

However, the Polo Grounds had seen better days by the time the Titans pulled into town.

"I don't know why anybody didn't break a leg in the Polo Grounds," said Booker Edgerson, the Bills' defensive back. "There were holes all over. To me, the field itself was terrible. Everyone was saying how bad War Memorial Stadium was. To me, it was a hell of a lot better than the Polo Grounds."

Grantham also found the Polo Grounds' field to be in desperate need of repair.

"Conditions kept going downhill all the time," he said. "They barely lined the field for football games, let alone practices. We just worked out there, and they didn't pay attention to the facilities. It was pretty bad."

The field was broadly uneven, to the point of distraction.

"One end zone had a slant down in toward the stands," Grantham said. "Quarterbacks would try to throw at the closed end of the stadium into the end zone, and the ball would go four to five feet over the receiver's head. We practiced for that on offense and defense."

Locker rooms were in an extraordinary state of disrepair.

"All the facilities were gone," Grantham said. "It was seldom we got hot water in the showers, and if you were not in there first, you wouldn't get it. We had problems getting towels and equipment, and there were rats in the locker room."

Eastern AFL teams didn't have a monopoly on bad conditions.

"In Oakland, the stadium was not a stadium," Dawson said of one of three fields used by the Raiders. "It was Youell Field, along an expressway. And they had bleacher seats like in a high school, and the locker room was like a Quonset-hut thing slapdashed together. To get to the field, you had to walk through the crowd. Not that there were too many fans back then."

Players walking into a locker room expected to see lockers at the very least—but not at Frank Youell Field. There, players were forced to hang their clothes on pegs scattered along the wall that substituted for lockers.

The locker room at Youell Field was so small that coaches would hold their meetings in the end zone.

"A few more people crowded into there, and the walls were going to bust," said Al Locasale, longtime executive with the Raiders.

Jeppesen Stadium in Houston, originally opened as a field for area high schools in 1942, didn't have that kind of problem. The AFL's Houston Oilers faced other issues at Jeppesen, one of their two "home" stadiums.

"They would have high schools play on Friday nights—Texas high school football being so big—and then maybe somebody played there on Saturday and then the Oilers on Sunday," remembered Dawson. "You can imagine what the field was like by then."

The Chargers first played in the Los Angeles Coliseum before moving to San Diego, where they played in Balboa Stadium. Morris described it as "basically a high school stadium."

Chargers owner Barron Hilton described Balboa as "very inadequate. It had cement seats, and if anyone spilled any beer, everyone else got it on their tails. Balboa Stadium was not a major league stadium in any sense of the word."

Sometimes, playing football in a stadium made for baseball was like trying to fit a round peg into a square hole.

When the Dallas Texans moved to Kansas City after the 1962 season and became the Chiefs, they first played in Municipal Stadium, where Charley Finley's Athletics played baseball.

Tommy Brooker, the Chiefs' kicker, said it was not easy playing in the stadium, especially when the "baseball field came down in late October. It was a mess, but they had a guy who grew grass like in a week."

The transformation from baseball to football made strange bedfellows.

"When they would turn that field a certain way, it would wind up being like an L-shaped stadium and had bleachers on one side and both teams on the same sideline, which was kind of strange and different," Brooker recalled. "[Chiefs] coach [Hank] Stram and [Oakland Raiders coach] John Madden would be yelling and screaming on the same sideline, and we didn't have much love for each other during games."

Dawson remembered that the temporary bleachers were located right behind the two teams' player benches and were "basically the best seats in the house. They would pack them in there, and I always wonder if you were in the middle, how do you get out to go to a restroom and get back before the end of the game?"

While bad field conditions seemed to be the norm around the AFL in the early days, Dawson felt that Municipal Stadium in Kansas City received better care than most any other in the league.

"I remember George Toma did the fields for us, and the league eventually hired him because he was so great at keeping the fields in shape," Dawson said. "If a bunch of turf came up, his crew would go out on the field during a stop in play and fix it. That was the only stadium in the AFL I know where they did that.

"When we went to Arrowhead [Stadium in Kansas City], Tommy Prothro was coaching the Chargers, and he was a big smoker, and George would follow him around with a big trash can. A lit cigarette butt would have burned up the [Astroturf] field when he dropped it."

Before moving from Dallas to Kansas City, the Texans played in the iconic Cotton Bowl in Dallas.

"The Cotton Bowl was, I guess, the best stadium early on," Dawson said. "But it also was a 75,000-seat stadium that had 8,000 people there to watch the games."

The Cotton Bowl had better luck drawing fans for college games—including usually a full house for the famed annual series between Oklahoma and Texas. Known as the "Red River Rivalry" for the river that flows between the two states, the classic is played during the Texas State Fair every year. Started in 1900 before moving to Dallas in 1932, the game is considered one of the greatest rivalries in American sports.

The Cotton Bowl has featured some of college football's most memorable moments—including the 1954 game when Alabama's Tommy Lewis leaped off the bench to tackle Rice's Dickey Moegle, who was on his way to a touchdown. The referee signaled "touchdown" even though Moegle was brought down by Lewis on the 42-yard line.

Out-of-date stadiums in desperate need of repair, lousy locker rooms, and terrible field conditions in most cases—an imperfect world that many AFL teams faced on a daily basis in their own stadiums in those days.

But it was home. And the players somehow found a way to work through all the challenges with a growing new league in desperate need of recognition.

Many players remembered their stadiums with a unique fondness and grew to love their oddball characteristics.

Shaw "loved playing in Buffalo," especially because of the fans.

"I will never say a bad word about War Memorial Stadium because it was different in that the fans were right close to the field, and it was the same fans that sat behind the bench year after year," Shaw said. "The people behind the bench were season-ticket holders. They knew us, our wives, our children. We knew them, and if they weren't at a game, we would ask, 'Where is Sally, Sue, or Jim?' It was that kind of atmosphere—a real family atmosphere."

Parking space was limited around War Memorial Stadium. Without asking permission, Shaw parked his car in the front yard of a house across the street whenever he played a home game.

That led to a personal story that happened long after his retirement,

"I lived in a small town in Georgia called Toccoa—10,000 people—and we had a black family that moved next door to us. After a couple of weeks, I went over and introduced myself to the family, to welcome them to our community, and they said, 'Oh, we know you, but you don't remember us.' And this was a family that was much older than we were.

"She said, 'Your name is Billy Shaw, and you played for the Bills.'

"And I said, 'Yes, Ma'am, that's right.'

"She said, 'You parked your car in our front yard for about five years.'

"They lived across the street from War Memorial Stadium, and I parked my car in their yard all those years, and they had moved from Buffalo to Toccoa, Georgia, right next door to me!"

Shaw could finally thank his neighbors who had allowed him to use their front lawn as a parking lot all those years.

A thank-you long overdue.

4

Colorful Coaches

Some of them molded players into Hall of Famers and teams into champions. Some were less brilliant, but far more entertaining.

Some remained with one franchise throughout the league's existence. Others had wanderlust.

Whether stylish or stodgy, these are the coaches who made the AFL memorable.

HANK STRAM

One man stands above all others in the AFL coaching pantheon: Hank Stram.

That's high praise considering that his peers included, at one time or another during the league's 10-year run, Paul Brown, Weeb Ewbank, Sid Gillman, and Lou Saban.

But Stram was the biggest winner of them all, leading the Dallas Texans/Kansas City Chiefs franchise to three AFL championships and victory in the final Super Bowl played between the AFL and the NFL before the merger. Stram went 85–44 in the AFL.

"He was one of the pioneers of the American Football League and someone I admired as a fan long before I had the opportunity to ever meet him," said Patriots owner Robert Kraft, who should recognize a successful coach, having worked with Bill Parcells, Pete Carroll, and Bill Belichick.

"He was responsible for doing a lot of the things in the '60s that teams are still using now," added Len Dawson, the quarterback who flourished under Stram's guidance—and, in turn, made Stram's innovations (the moving pocket, receivers in motion, offset running backs, and two tight ends) work smoothly.

Stram wasn't merely a masterful coach; he was one of the most colorful characters in a league full of them. A bon vivant in a day when most sideline bosses wore dull gray suits or topcoats, Stram could outdress opponents as well as outthink them.

Stram always had football on his mind—even while eating. At dinner in a restaurant, he would diagram plays on the napkins. Dawson said Stram was discouraged from returning to some eateries because he ruined the cloth napkins with drawings of naked screens and defensive line stunts.

Stram had a way with words, famously being caught in an NFL Films segment talking about "matriculating down the field." His engaging manner entranced the media, the fans, and, most important, the players.

"Hank had his own language," said longtime Chiefs executive Jack Steadman. "He had a name for everything. He was a funny guy. He had a great sense of humor. He worked really well . . . he was a brilliant coach. He just had a great mind for offense and defense.

"We had an unbelievable rivalry with San Diego because the two coaches, Gillman and Stram, were the two best coaches in the league. They went after each other."

Tactically, of course. Both were offensive wizards, but Stram, with his triple-stack defense, had an edge in that area. And he also was one of the first coaches to pay close attention to special teams.

Indeed, his interest in the kick teams led Stram to refine another of his creations. Stram found that his placekicker in the early seasons, Tommy Brooker, was an effective tight end, sparking the coach's perfecting the double-tight-end formation for which the Chiefs partly became renowned.

"I think the AFL brought something different to the game," said Brooker, who kicked the field goal to win the 1962 title game at Houston in double overtime. "Just like Coach Stram with the shifting, there were a lot of innovations the AFL should be remembered for.

"For a long time, Hank took credit for creating the two-tight-end system, whether that's true or not. But we used it and it was a very evasive system.

"But it also worked because Fred Arbanas and I would switch positions so one of us could catch our breath after running pass routes. I would also play in a split formation sometimes; we had enough formations that first year I was there that it would thoroughly confuse the defenses of other teams. And we would build on it."

Stram coached the Texans to the AFL championship in 1962, then led the Chiefs to league titles in the 1966 season and in 1969 before winning Super Bowl IV.

Stram built the Chiefs from scratch. An assistant coach at the University of Miami, Stram earlier had coached at Southern Methodist University, where Chiefs owner Lamar Hunt was a backup in his college days, so there was some familiarity. Not that Stram was Hunt's first coaching choice when he was putting together the Texans for their first season in 1960. When Hunt started the AFL, he looked at hiring some NFL head coaches or assistants to run the Texans but met with much resistance.

Obviously, someone willing to start up a new professional football league had no qualms about gambling on an unproven college coach who had never run his own team. So Hunt met with Stram, and, realizing that their visions for the franchise and the AFL itself were similar, he hired Stram.

"We were awfully lucky," Hunt said of Stram's hiring. "He had never been a head coach before, and you never know how that's going to work out."

Both Tom Landry and Bud Wilkinson had rejected the Texans' coaching job before Stram accepted. It turned out to be a perfect fit.

"I think Hank is really symbolic of the coaching style and the coaching personality of the American Football League," Hunt said. "Maybe he never would have gotten a chance anywhere else. Hank personified the American Football League. He was a salesman. He was an innovator. He wasn't afraid to try new things."

It all led the Chiefs to a special place in football history and personally for Stram, a spot in the Pro Football Hall of Fame.

How did Stram get to Canton?

Certainly thanks to a willingness to try anything on the football field. At a time when most NFL teams were copycats, sticking with conservative, run-oriented offenses even with the likes of John Unitas, Bart Starr, and Y. A. Tittle among its quarterbacks, AFL coaches were hell-bent for high-flying action.

None more so than Stram.

"Hank would do things different, and he would always have a reason for what he was doing," Dawson said. "His mind was always going as to how he could help his team get better. Hank was the first coach to start creating a variety of formations."

Such as his famed tight-I formation, with both receivers pulled in next to the tackles and the tight end setting up in all kinds of places: behind the quarterback, in a slotback spot, or split out a few yards.

"He would create a formation to make the defense move instead of letting them get set."

Stram made neutralizing an opponent's best defender a priority. Ask the Chicago Bears, who played the Chiefs in an exhibition game in the 1967 preseason.

For Stram, it was more than a meaningless warm-up game. Outside of the previous Super Bowl, in which Kansas City lost to Green Bay, it was the Chiefs' first meeting with an NFL club. Stram treated it like a divisional game in December.

The Bears' fearsome defense was led by Dick Butkus, one of the greatest middle linebackers in pro football history. The way the Chiefs played it, Butkus was completely ineffective.

"They had a strong-side tackle and weak-side tackle, and where the [Bears'] linebackers and safeties lined up was all predicated on where our tight end went," Dawson recalled. "The tight end dictated which was the strong side."

Stram put his tight end, usually Arbanas, just about everywhere but snapping the ball. It bewildered the Chiefs' opponents.

"They would have to guess where he was going," Dawson said. "Whichever direction they went, I would send the tight end the other way. It gave us the advantage.

"So they had their other linebackers running into Butkus in the middle; they didn't know what to do. And they are thinking about that rather than their responsibilities."

Kansas City won 66–24.

Not only could Stram coach a good game, he could talk one. Some remembered lines:

"Yesterday is a canceled check. Today is cash on the line. Tomorrow is a promissory note."

"You can't be fat and fast, too; so lift, run, diet, and work. You cannot win if you cannot run."

"Let's matriculate the ball down the field, boys."

That last one was a highlight of the NFL Films special on Super Bowl IV. Stram was the first coach to wear a wireless microphone during a championship game, and he did it secretly, insisting that nobody be told just in case he flopped. In fact, he asked for final approval of the film, which also featured his repetitive mantra, "65 toss power trap," the running play used by Mike Garrett to score a touchdown.

As the Chiefs began dominating the action, Stram became more verbal and more confident, and he strode up and down the sideline with a rolled-up game plan in his hand.

"I didn't really look at it," Stram said of the papers he carried. "I knew what we were going to do. I used to tell people it was a list to bring groceries home for Phyllis."

The minidocumentary became a classic.

Stram also would try out anyone for his team, although he was more hit or miss with his personnel decisions than his game plans (more on that later).

"My philosophy was to get the best players and then try to do something new with them," Stram said.

That included bringing in players from historically black schools.

One of his biggest hits was linebacker Willie Lanier out of Morgan State, hardly a football factory.

"He didn't care what color you were, he wanted to win," Dawson said. "The AFL had guys like Lloyd Wells, a scout who went to all these [mainly black] schools to find players, and that was how we got Willie Lanier here."

Dawson and Lanier believe that the family atmosphere that Stram created immediately was conducive to winning. It didn't hurt having an owner like Hunt, whom Brooker called "one of the guys," overseeing the Chiefs.

"He was really sincere when he talked about the team being a family," Dawson said of Stram.

Added Lanier, "All of us had a great joy in being able to experience the sport at the level we did because of his creative mind and the kind of personality that he put around you. That allowed everyone to perform at levels higher than they would have without him."

Steadman recalls that Stram could be too loyal, which eventually haunted the Chiefs when they became part of the AFC.

"I hired Don Klosterman as our scout, a talent scout out of San Diego," Steadman said. "And he really was responsible for building our championship teams in the sixties. And then after he was hired by Houston as their general manager, Hank wanted to take over the scouting and do the player contracts as well. And we were building a stadium, a sports complex in Kansas City, and my time was really tied up with stadium projects.

"So Lamar and I agreed to give Hank more responsibility. That turned out to be a bad decision looking back on it because Hank would keep the old players. We just weren't bringing in good talent to replace the older players. They just got old."

But Stram's coaching skills never did—even when he moved on later to the New Orleans Saints in the NFC. He always stayed fresh, his innovative mind working, as he continued to pursue his lifelong passion.

"I know it meant everything to him because all he wanted to do was be a coach," Dawson said. "He had the ability to make each and every one of us feel special. I wear a Super Bowl ring on this hand and a Hall of Fame ring on this one, and it's all because of Hank Stram."

SID GILLMAN

No one is more responsible for the emergence of the passing game as the key weapon—and attraction—in pro football than Sid Gillman.

Al Davis? Coached under Gillman.

Bill Walsh? Studied Gillman's principles.

John Hadl and Lance Alworth? Played for the man.

Simply put, Gillman was the originator of the modern passing game, be it the West Coast offense and its multiple variations, the motion attack, or the varied downfield routes and timing patterns being used today.

"Absolutely, without question," former Chiefs president Carl Peterson said. "Sid was a true giant in our business. He was probably the most innovative offensive mind in our game."

To Gillman, the guys who threw the ball and the ones who caught and ran with it were the backbone of the sport.

"The big play comes with the pass," he would say. "God bless those runners because they get you the first down, give you ball control, and keep your defense off the field. But if you want to ring the cash register, you have to pass."

So Gillman's teams passed . . . and passed . . . and passed.

Gillman became the Chargers' first head coach in 1960, bringing along perhaps the best credentials among all the AFL's original coaches. Gillman played at Ohio State under legendary coach Francis Schmidt, whose nickname was "Shut the Gates of Mercy." He moved on to several assistant coaching jobs in college and was the head man at Miami of Ohio—considered the cradle of coaches in college football—and the University of Cincinnati.

When he got to the pros, Gillman began putting his offensive theories to work with the Rams, who went to the 1955 NFL championship game in his first season in Los Angeles. But when the team crashed to a 2–10 record in 1959, he was fired.

Barron Hilton, one of the AFL's founding fathers, sought out Gillman almost immediately. And in the AFL, Gillman truly put his offensive philosophies into action—without mercy.

He was helped by the likes of Davis and Chuck Noll, Joe Madro, and Jack Faulkner.

"He was so far ahead of his time, people couldn't totally understand what he was doing," said Walsh, considered the inventor of the West Coast offense. "He was one of the great offensive minds in football history. There's a lineage between Sid Gillman and what you see on the field today."

Gillman was an immediate success with the Chargers, first in Los Angeles in 1960, when they won the Western Division before losing to Houston in the title game, and then in San Diego for the rest of the AFL's existence. The first coach to win divisions in the NFL and AFL, Gillman led the Chargers to the 1963 league crown and won five division championships in all.

And they were the forerunner of the prolific aerial attacks later seen with the Raiders and Cowboys, 49ers and Vikings, and Rams and Patriots. In Gillman's first nine full seasons at the helm, the Chargers never scored fewer than 314 points in 12 games and reached as high as 399.

"He was way ahead of his time in organization, in the passing game, and offensive football," Davis said. "In the '60s, the passing game was not yet really developed. At the advent of the AFL, certainly the Chargers were the flagship for all teams to emulate.

"Sid Gillman was the father of modern-day passing. It had been thought of as vertical, the length of the field, but Sid also thought of it as horizontal. Sid used the width of the field."

His teams were able to do so because of the talent Gillman procured. Whether it was Jack Kemp or Hadl, he always had the trigger man at quarterback. He had versatile running backs such as Paul Lowe and Keith Lincoln and brilliant receivers in Lance Alworth and Gary Garrison. And nonpareil coaching staffs.

"I give all the credit to Sid," Hilton said. "Sid was an outstanding coach who really had a great recruiting style with the people he hired. Al Davis and our staff, when they really went after top ballplayers, they got them. And he was the general manager after Frank Leahy retired. He surely had a great eye for talent, starting with the staff and his assistant coaches."

Legend has it that Gillman, while working as a movie theater usher, would take home football segments of the newsreels and watch them on his own projector, which he bought for $15. No one who knew him doubted that he did that.

"Sid lived and breathed football, and he'd watch film for hours and run it backward and forward in the late hours, watching every play and determining which players he wanted to retain and which players couldn't make the club," Hilton added. "He also was structuring plays he thought would be effective."

Among the offensive principles Gillman espoused that have become staples of modern football are the following:

The use of film study of opponents

Timing routes in which the quarterback throws the ball to a spot the receiver is supposed to reach at a specific time during a play

Using four and even five receivers to spread the field

Motion on offense, which other coaches such as Hank Stram would take to a higher level

Having quarterbacks "bounce" on their feet while surveying the field, giving them a better feel for a play's development (Gillman always believed that a flat-footed passer was a passer about to be sacked)

"I hate like hell to have something happen on a football field that I am not familiar with or that I haven't seen," Gillman said. "Any time I see a good idea, it goes on a sheet. I collect ideas.

"Football has evolved into a game of looks. It's not the number of plays but taking one play and running it from eight, nine, 10 different formations, in both the passing game and the running game. In the old days, coaches would pride themselves on the number of plays they'd run. You would hear about a coach that has 500 plays. That's gone, dead and buried."

Gillman had what he called the "Dirty Dozen."

"We'd take a dozen plays and run two dozen formations. That helped us by cutting down practice times and not have to work on so many different thoughts. No matter how smart or great a player or team is, you don't want to load them down with too much."

Hadl, the engineer of so many offensive jolts by the Chargers, never felt loaded down. More like privileged being Gillman's quarterback.

"Detroit drafted me number 1 as a running back, and the Chargers drafted me number 3 and wanted me to be a quarterback," Hadl said. "I went to San Diego and saw that city. What a fabulous place that was. Sid Gillman wanted me to be a quarterback. If I was going to make it, I wanted to make it as a quarterback.

"What I was asked to do was a 180-degree change from what I did at Kansas. I truly had to learn how to throw the football as far as proper technique, setup, foot position. But I was a good enough athlete that I caught on pretty fast."

Hadl referred to Gillman as "an offensive genius."

"His goal was for me to understand the offense as well as he did. And that's exactly what happened. I knew it so well that Sid and I would occasionally butt heads over play calling."

Hadl certainly had the perfect teacher—one who appropriately entered the Pro Football Hall of Fame in 1983 along with Sonny Jurgensen, Paul Warfield, and Bobby Mitchell, three of the greatest offensive forces in football history.

LOU SABAN

Few coaches led a more nomadic life than Lou Saban, which seems appropriate because Saban guided three AFL franchises in the league's decade of existence.

Along with the debuting Patriots in 1960, the Bills and the Broncos (in the AFL and the NFL), Saban also worked the sidelines at nearly a dozen colleges. The only head coach for three AFL clubs, Saban won back-to-back titles with the Bills in 1964–1965, and after his four-year stint with the Broncos, he returned to western New York for a bit more than four seasons.

A man for all football seasons at any venue.

"I've coached at all levels, covered the gamut, and I've never really seen any difference," Saban once said. "My coaching techniques are pretty much the same, with some adjustments for what younger players can and can't do."

What Saban could—and wanted—to do most was teach, which was why he always seemed to stray back to the college level. But he had plenty of opportunity to guide and sculpt and educate in the AFL.

"He was one of the great coaches from the early days of the American Football League, along with Sid Gillman, Al Davis, and Hank Stram," said AFL quarterbacking great Jack Kemp. "Coach Saban's leadership is what set the stage for our Buffalo Bills' AFL championships in 1964 and 1965."

Added Bills receiver Ed Rutkowski, "He knew how to press that button in all of us and how to get the best out of us. I remember when we had our first two wide receivers go down—Elbert Dubenion and I don't know who the other one was—I had to go in with Glenn Bass.

"I think the first game I was going to start in place of Dubenion was against the Jets. So I stayed after practice to work on my pass routes and everything else. The Thursday before the game, which was on Sunday, I'm walking off the field after practice, and coach comes over to me and says, 'You know, Ed, whether we win or not depends on your performance.'

"I said, 'What do you mean?'

"'Well, this game rests on you. You better have a hell of a game, otherwise we're going to lose.'

"Well, I was all fired up. I had one of the best games of my life. And I found out years later at one of our reunions that he said the exact same thing to Glenn Bass."

Saban was a standout quarterback and linebacker at Indiana before joining the Cleveland Browns of the All-America Football Conference (AAFC). Saban was an all-AAFC selection while starring for the Browns from 1946 to 1949.

Saban began his roving career in 1950 as head coach at Case Institute of Technology in Cleveland. He moved to Northwestern in 1955, going 0–8–1, hardly a harbinger of his coaching prowess.

But at Western Illinois, Saban had three winning seasons, including a 9–0 campaign in 1959.

Then it was off to Beantown.

"As the Patriots' first head coach, Lou helped kick off a new era of football in Boston," current Patriots owner Robert Kraft said on Saban's death in 2009. "This season, we will be celebrating the Patriots' fiftieth anniversary and reflecting back on that inaugural season. It should give us all cause to appreciate Lou's many contributions during the Patriots' formative years."

Actually, those contributions were minimal compared to Saban's work in Buffalo and Denver, but they were significant nonetheless.

The Patriots were one of the financially strapped franchises at the outset of the AFL. While they weren't exactly operating on a shoestring, there were limitations that the Chargers, Oilers, and Texans, for example, didn't have.

So the price tag for a head coach could have been a stumbling block, but Saban wasn't an expensive commodity.

And he had enough connections—plus a convincing manner—to build a representative roster. One of the first players he grabbed from the college ranks was multifaceted Larry Garron, who had played for Saban at Western Illinois.

Garron was one of a half dozen original Patriots who would have a big impact in the AFL. Gino Cappelletti, Jim Colclough, Bobby Dee, Tom Addison, Ron Burton, Bob Yates, Ross O'Hanley, Jack Rudolph, Chuck Shonta, and Tom Stephens all learned under Saban and lasted at least four seasons in Boston.

Unfortunately, Saban remained for only 19 games with the Patriots, going 7–12. The team would flourish in the next few years under Mike Holovak—and with many of the players Saban brought aboard—but Saban already was on to his next port of call: not-so-balmy Buffalo.

Saban joined the Bills in 1962 and had four winning seasons, two of them gloriously triumphant. For those who only recall the Bills' flops in four straight Super Bowls—never mind how impressive just making four consecutive Super Bowls is—there are two AFL championship trophies residing in Buffalo.

Saban brought them there.

"It all came together under Lou Saban," said Booker Edgerson, a starter for all of Saban's tenure in Buffalo, when the cornerback had 16 interceptions. "One thing about Saban, if you weren't doing a good job, he'd take you out of the game. If Jack Kemp was having a bad game, snatch him, and put Daryle Lamonica in there. And if Daryle wasn't doing good, he'd take him out and put Kemp back in. That's what Lou Saban did. He said it's all about winning, it's not about who's playing first string and who did this and who did that."

Edgerson remembered his rookie year in Buffalo when Saban shuffled a great number of new players in and out of camp, even during the exhibition season. It made the players nervous.

"The guys felt uneasy with it," Edgerson recalled. "They said, 'We don't know if we're making the team or not.' So the guys had a meeting and discussed it, and they went to Saban.

"'Look, Coach, we're out there busting our butt and doing [everything you ask], and you keep bringing guys in and out of here. We're not comfortable.'

"And Saban said, 'Look, I'm not comfortable with the way you guys are playing. I tell you what: I'm going to fire some people before they fire me.' And that's just the way it was. Saban was a man's man. He played the game hard, and he was a great coach and a great mentor on my end. I'm quite sure he mentored a lot of other guys, too."

One of them was Kemp, who came over from San Diego already a star, and during his six seasons as a Bill was as good as George Blanda, Len Dawson, John Hadl, and Joe Namath. In a league that featured outstanding passers, Kemp stood out, particularly in the AFL's earliest years.

Saban got the better of Gillman in bringing Kemp to western New York.

"Jack Kemp would kind of get me from time to time that he was traded to the Bills for $100," recalled original Chargers owner Barron Hilton, "and I would remind him it was Sid's decision to put him up for $100 and that Saban moved quickly.

"Jack fractured his finger on a helmet of an oncoming lineman, and Sid believed Jack wouldn't recover from that. Jack went to a doctor to have the finger examined, and he took a football with him and said to the doctor, 'I want you to set this finger on the profile of the football,' which he did.

"Of course, Buffalo picked him up, and Jack had outstanding years in Buffalo and won two championships."

With Kemp aboard and despite the blistering cold and wicked winds that whipped through War Memorial Stadium, Saban set about balancing an offense that had a man mountain of a running back in Cookie Gilchrist.

"Lou knew that Cookie could gain 1,000 yards or more and that he was tough near the goal line," Kemp said. "He also knew that defenses would gang up on Cookie if we couldn't throw and that we had the weapons to throw the football."

To throw it, Kemp needed the time to survey the field and find his receivers. So Saban concentrated on building a staunch offensive line, and he already had the best building block (or blocker) in Billy Shaw.

Shaw was a second-round draft pick from Georgia Tech in 1961, the year before Saban arrived. He moved directly into the starting lineup at left guard and eventually was joined by a superb group of linemen that was the backbone of a diversified attack. It had to be that way.

Saban insisted that every block be the right block and that every running back make the correct cut. No quarterback could hold the ball too long or launch it to the wrong receiver.

"Lou was always looking for perfection—and he just had a vision from his viewpoint on the sidelines," said Shaw, the only Pro Football Hall of Fame member to play his entire career in the AFL. "And Lou was a very, very intelligent person, and he could see things on the field.

"Most of the negative comments came not after the game but the next day in the film room, on Tuesday. We'd play on Sunday. He wouldn't bother us on Monday; that was our day off. But Tuesday was film day."

That was when the Bills found out how poorly they played, even in victory. Saban usually had a laundry list of mistakes ready and read the riot act to his team.

"We knew that the end result was that we won, but how in the world did we make so many mistakes and win?" Shaw said. "He saw all of that as we were playing and as the game was going on, and so he had a transcript already ready for Tuesday morning's film.

"Yeah, there were some times that you wondered if you won or lost."

Mostly, Saban's Bills won.

In their first four seasons under Saban, they went 36–17–3. The only year they didn't make the playoffs was Saban's first, 1962. They won the AFL title in his final two seasons in Buffalo, both times beating San Diego, 20–7 at home and 23–0 at Balboa Stadium.

"He was like a father to me," Edgerson said. "He steered me in the right direction. He gave me advice. Some of it, I didn't like, but isn't that what a father does?

"He was a good man. You could believe him. He was a good coach, and I thought he treated everybody the same. He was a great motivator. He could give you a pep talk. He used to tell me, 'If you don't catch the ball, I'm going to cut you.' That was motivation enough for me."

Yet Saban wasn't motivated to remain in Buffalo, and the reasons are murky.

Bills owner Ralph Wilson has said that Saban longed to return to college ball. Others retorted that Saban was miffed over a reduction in his responsibilities and the lack of a long-term contract.

Regardless, Saban headed to the University of Maryland. But after one distressing season as head coach of the Terrapins, Saban was back in the AFL, this time with Denver—and with a lengthy deal.

Saban signed a 10-year contract as both coach and general manager of the Broncos, a franchise that experienced no glory days before he arrived. In fact, the Broncos often were underfinanced and always underachieving. Their 7–7 mark in 1962 was their best season by far.

Saban would not reverse those fortunes, going a dismal 3–11 in his first year as the Broncos' coach. In his five seasons leading the Broncos, they were 20–42–3 before he was dismissed nine games (and six defeats) into the 1971 season, replaced by Jerry Smith.

During his Denver tenure, though, Saban brought in such skilled players as Floyd Little, Jim Turner, Rich Jackson, Paul Smith, Billy Thompson, Bob Anderson, Lyle Alzado, Marv Montgomery, Billy Masters, and Charles Greer. All were key parts of the foundation of the organization that Saban built and instrumental in the Broncos' future successes.

Saban never could reproduce his greatest pro football success, not even when Wilson was persuaded to hire him back in 1972 for another four-plus seasons. But Saban was influential far beyond the football field, too.

Indeed, one of pro sports' most accomplished figures, New York Yankees owner George Steinbrenner, owed some of his success to

Saban. Steinbrenner was a receivers coach at Northwestern under Saban in 1955.

"He has been my friend and mentor for over 50 years and one of the people who helped shape my life," Steinbrenner said when Saban died. "Lou was tough and disciplined, and he earned all the respect and recognition that came his way. He spent a lifetime leading, teaching, and inspiring and took great satisfaction in making the lives around him better."

WEEB EWBANK

The name alone should be memorable; how many Weebs have you ever known?

Yet when he came to coach New York's AFL entry in 1963, one sportscaster called him Ewb Weebank. Certainly a coach who had led Baltimore to two straight NFL championships, both against the local Giants no less, should have been better recognized and more accurately referenced in the Big Apple.

Then again, Ewbank—real first name Wilbur, which his younger brother could not pronounce, thus Weeb—was joining a franchise that was almost totally ignored while it was the New York Titans. Now they were the Jets, but they remained saddled in the dilapidated Polo Grounds for one more year before heading to Shea Stadium.

So even if the team seemed bedraggled once more, the Jets actually were ready to soar under new management led by aggressive entrepreneur Sonny Werblin.

Ewbank was recommended to Werblin by Jimmy Cannon, the renowned sportswriter and columnist in New York. The Colts had just fired Ewbank, and Werblin did some quick and thorough research, talked to his fellow owners, and grabbed Ewbank before another team could hire him.

On the day Werblin made the announcement, the team name was changed to Jets.

Following front-office turmoil resulting in bounced checks and rotating rosters, Ewbank would bring stability to one of the AFL's key franchises.

In a few years, he'd also help bring equality to the upstart league.

"Weeb was a great coach and a great organizer," said Hall of Fame receiver Don Maynard, who was with the Giants when Ewbank's

Colts beat them for the 1958 title in the first professional overtime game ever. "He kept things in perspective. I don't think we ever worked out more than two hours. He could get more done in two hours than most coaches could in four.

"When [Joe] Namath came along, we'd get out there with [Pete] Lammons, [George] Sauer, and Bake Turner and work 20 to 30 minutes on the passing game. Weeb let us put in some secret plays. He let me implement a lot of things. We were the first team that used routes where the quarterback threw the ball real early in the play.

"We were always on the same page. In eight years, I can only remember one busted play."

Ewbank's strength was offense, but he also was great at delegating authority. He let Walt Michaels run the defense, only rarely getting involved with that unit.

"The only time Weeb came over on our side of the ball is if we gave up a bunch of points," said Larry Grantham, an original Jet and the defensive leader throughout Ewbank's tenure. "He was never into Xs and Os on the defensive side of the ball.

"He made a statement when he came in to New York that I was playing with shoulder pads he wouldn't let a junior high team wear. But he gave us our room to do what we did best."

A squat, roundish man at times referred to as a troll, a munchkin, or even a fire hydrant, Ewbank stood tall among his peers. The only coach to guide teams in the AFL and NFL to championships, Ewbank's brilliance on the sideline led to his Pro Football Hall of Fame induction in 1978.

And if there's any doubt about Ewbank's acumen, consider that he was mentor to John Unitas and Namath, two of his colleagues in Canton.

"It started out I really wanted to play for Weeb because of what Weeb accomplished with the Colts and with Johnny Unitas," Namath said. "[Alabama] Coach [Bear] Bryant said, 'Joe, you've got to learn the game on that level, and the people you work with is most important.'

"We had talked about Coach Ewbank's success at Baltimore, and working with Johnny Unitas carried so much weight. He basically talked about the good parts of Coach Ewbank's coaching."

Which were?

"What made him special for us was his knowledge of the game and what we needed to do to get the job done," Namath said. "I took a liking to him early when he insisted on excellent pass protection. He understood what went through a quarterback's mind, he understood the problems you have, seeing things and staying with things and reading defenses. He was never afraid.

"I used to marvel at him when he wanted to run a play that seemed a little hairy. He showed respect for other teams but never showed an ounce of fear for other teams. He respected their abilities and knew what they were capable of. He always pumped us up and always had us thinking we were going to win."

Ewbank didn't win a lot early on in Baltimore, going 20–27–1 before leading the Colts to their 1958 and 1959 NFL titles. With the Jets, the numbers were similar over a five-year stretch at the start: 29–35–6.

But Werblin was being patient with Ewbank, who in his first two seasons didn't have Namath on the squad. Ewbank's draft choices, though, were impressive, featuring players who would contribute to the Jets' rise—Matt Snell, Gerry Philbin, Dave Herman, Ralph Baker, Verlon Biggs, Emerson Boozer, George Sauer, and Lammons. His selections during the AFL–NFL bidding wars were just as farsighted, even if the likes of John Mackey, Jerry Stovall, Willie Richardson, Johnny Roland, and Ken Bowman wound up starring elsewhere.

The Jets probably should have made the playoffs for the first time in 1967 but blew three of their final four games to lose the East race to Houston. Still, there was a sense that Ewbank was overseeing something special heading into 1968.

"We didn't have any defense when we got Joe," said longtime Jets publicist Frank Ramos. "For a long time, it was like that, actually. We were 5–8–1 on a regular basis. We knew you had to build everything around him."

In 1967, Namath had a breakout year—throwing for 4,000 yards and 26 touchdowns in 14 games.

"In 1968 we finally had a good defense," Ramos said. "We felt very confident about being good enough to win the championship when that year started."

The Jets had not only Broadway Joe but also tremendous leadership and experience in other areas.

The offensive line featured the likes of Herman, John Schmitt, and Winston Hill; the backfield Boozer and Snell; and the receiving corps Maynard, Sauer, and Lammons.

Anchoring the defensive line were Philbin, John Elliott, and Biggs. The Jets were also strong at the linebacker position with Grantham, Al Atkinson, and Baker, who were teammates for many seasons. Safety was in good hands too, with Jim Hudson.

"Hudson was a really underrated strong safety," Ramos said. "In Walt Michaels's defense, he would play Hudson on the line of scrimmage like a linebacker. Walt was the first guy to come up with the idea of special guys to be pass rushers.

"Our kicker, Jim Turner, was so accurate, he hardly ever missed, even though he often had to kick on bad fields. He just couldn't kick off, didn't have the big leg. So Biggs, who hated to kick off because it meant he would get hit by blockers, would do it. Or [punter] Curley Johnson would tie up his punting shoe and go out and kick off."

All of it was overseen by Ewbank, who gave his stamp of approval to the innovations that his assistants—and sometimes his players—came up with.

What Ewbank might best be remembered for is, of course, how he handled Namath's guarantee before the 1969 Super Bowl meeting with Weeb's former team, the Colts. At the outset, in fact, Ewbank didn't handle it very well at all.

Ewbank was upset—beyond upset.

"Coach Ewbank said they would put that up there [on the bulletin board], and it would give them extra incentive, and I laughed," Namath said. "I said, 'If they need clippings for the bulletin board, they are in trouble.'

"He told me to behave myself from there on. He knew I could dig a big hole for myself, so he said, 'Don't say anything from here on in.' He made me become a little wary of what I would say.

"I honest to God felt bad he was upset about it."

Then the Jets pulled off the biggest upset in pro football history, designed by Weeb and engineered by Joe Willie.

Ewbank might have had a secure place in pro football history and perhaps a spot in the Hall of Fame, even without Super Bowl III.

"One thing that really stands out about Weeb," Ramos said, "think about some of the most important games in the history of pro football, and Weeb was involved."

When the 1950 Browns came into the NFL from the AAFC, they were made to play the Philadelphia Eagles right away and beat the NFL's defending champions. Ewbank was in charge of pass protection and defensive tackles for the Browns.

"Then, of course, he had the 1958 sudden-death game [between the Colts and Giants].

"Then the Super Bowl in 1969, the most important of them all."

Ewbank would add to his legacy when he coached in the first *Monday Night Football* game on the first weekend of regular-season play between the merged leagues.

Indeed, Ewbank's role in the sport is as significant and influential as that of Paul Brown, Sid Gillman, Hank Stram, and other memorable mentors in the AFL.

"One of the best coaches that ever lived, ever coached the game of football," Namath said of Ewbank's legacy.

"At times, you wonder why a coach does things or how. I've said this before: With every new coach I played for, Weeb got better and better. He had something very special, and one thing he shared with all of us was winning championships."

He did it in New York and did it in Baltimore.

"People will never forget that," Namath said. "Without Weeb, I don't believe we would have done it."

PAUL BROWN

By the time Paul Brown officially became an AFL owner, his legend was established—in two other leagues.

Brown was the first coach of the Cleveland franchise in the AAFC but did not own the club. And no, he was not vain enough to name the team in his honor: Cleveland fans chose the name in a newspaper contest because Paul Brown was a tremendously popular figure in Ohio from his coaching roles at Washington High School in Massillon and then at Ohio State.

Under Brown, Cleveland won all four of the AAFC's championships from 1946 to 1949. Then the NFL came calling, grabbing the Browns, Los Angeles Rams, and San Francisco 49ers in the original "merger."

And Cleveland's success didn't abate a bit when it joined the establishment. The Browns won the NFL crown in their debut season, then went to three more title games in a row, losing each, before adding two more league championships.

Even though the Browns remained a contender, the coach's job became tenuous soon after Art Modell bought the team in 1961. Two years later, Paul Brown was fired.

"Coach Brown did not want the players to know how he really felt about that, but you could not have quoted him as saying the name Art Modell," former Bengals center Bob Johnson said with a laugh.

Modell's dismissal of Brown would not be the final step in his coaching career. No way would the proud Brown let such an ignominious development signify the end.

He soon was in discussions with Ohio governor James Rhodes about bringing an AFL expansion team to Cincinnati. When the city council approved construction plans for a new stadium for baseball's Reds and Brown's new team, AFL owners—eager to have Brown within their ranks—readily agreed to the entry of a tenth franchise in 1968. The Miami Dolphins had become the AFL's ninth team when the league expanded for the first time in the 1966 season.

"We picked Cincinnati because my father was an Ohio guy," said Bengals president Mike Brown, who has run the team since his father's death in 1991. "He was born and raised in Ohio, went to high school and college in Ohio, and coached at Massillon, coached at Ohio State, and with the Browns. These were the people he knew best. We came here for that reason.

"The town was very interested in getting a team; it was a feather in the cap of the city for a pro team to come here, and that excited people, and they wanted to be part of it. The reception was very good at the start here."

It certainly didn't hurt to have a Hall of Fame coach in charge, either.

And there was no mistaking who was in charge with the Bengals.

"You know, a complete authority figure in football works well. It's what players want," said Johnson, the Bengals' first draft pick. "As soon as a coach doesn't have what it takes to control a player's destiny, he will fail.

"And you always knew he was in charge and that he cared [about you]. We noticed that he paid attention to everyone in practice. There is something to be said about the boss being the boss. He laid down the law: 'If you have a dispute, there is no one to go to except to me. So don't pretend to go around me or to another owner or anyone.'"

Two examples of Brown's handling of players during the Bengals' AFL days: Jesse Phillips and Teddy Washington. Phillips would play five seasons for the team, while Washington wouldn't get out of his first.

Mike Brown remembered that his father took a chance on Phillips even though he had just finished a jail term.

"I welcomed Jesse Philips out of prison, literally," Mike Brown said. "We brought him back to the team in Ohio. He was in prison for having run off with somebody's radio set, I believe. A tough judge put him, a young guy from Michigan State, into jail.

"But he was a good player for us. Al Davis always coveted him after he ran about 80 yards versus the Raiders."

Johnson noted that Paul Brown could provide players with tough love and guidance.

"Paul Brown believed in him," Johnson said of Phillips. "He would take players and give them a clean sheet."

In the case of Washington, Paul Brown was just plain tough. Washington was a running back out of San Diego State who quickly learned a hard lesson from Brown.

"Teddy missed a practice one time, and just before we were heading for the plane to go to a game, Coach Brown asked Teddy where he was, and Teddy said he overslept," Johnson remembered. "Coach Brown told him, 'Get off my plane.'

"That said something to all the other players, that Coach Brown just pitched him [off the team]. It makes you square up. It makes a team square up. He wasn't going to allow any problem players when it had to do with the team. He wanted an unselfish player, a team-first guy, because if that is the attitude and you work hard, it is contagious."

As a side note, it turned out in later years that Washington would be the father of Rashaan Salaam, the Heisman Trophy winner in 1994.

So the Bengals worked hard under Brown, believing that winning soon would become contagious. By year 3, the first season in the NFL, Cincinnati won the AFC Central.

The Bengals would make the playoffs twice more under Brown before he retired from coaching after the 1975 season.

"I did think that core of people were team people and cared about the team and worked their butts off," Johnson said. "And that's how you get something started and make it successful.

"Coach Brown would walk up to the podium and tell the team, 'The only things we do as a staff is talk about you guys.' But he meant not only how we played football, but how do you spend your money, what kind of person are you? He would challenge people to be the 'right kind of person for the team.'"

In 1970, Brown also challenged the other 25 team owners. He adamantly insisted that three NFL teams be moved into the AFC before interleague play began that year—as per the agreement from 1966.

Most of the established NFL clubs wanted to keep the 16–10 makeup of 1969, in part because many of the hard-liners from the NFL had no interest in moving over to a conference they considered inferior.

And then there were the AFL hard-liners.

"We had as part of our franchise agreement that there would be realignment," Mike Brown said. "My father had been involved with the Browns when they were in the All-America Football Conference when it merged with the NFL, three teams coming in: Baltimore, Cleveland, and San Francisco.

"He had lived through this kind of thing and felt strongly—and, I felt, correctly—that the league should be one league."

Paul Brown had to fight not only against the AFL people who were very proud of their accomplishment and liked being separate—Al Davis would be one of them—but also against an NFL that did not want to recognize that they were an equal.

"Those NFL people were quite content with 16–10," Mike Brown said, referring to the 16 NFL teams remaining together in a new conference called the NFC and the 10 AFL teams in the AFC. "We made the argument that our merger agreement would not permit that 16–10; they had promised us as part of our deal that there would be realignment, and we stood on that."

Edward Bennett Williams, owner of the Washington Redskins, was one of the NFL hard-liners. At one meeting, he stood up and said there wasn't a court in the country that would support the AFL's position.

"That carried a lot of conviction with those guys."

But obviously not enough to preserve the 16–10 split desired by many NFL owners.

"Finally, they agreed there would be realignment," Mike Brown said.

But there was another issue: which three teams would come over to the newly formed AFC from the NFL?

"There was a famous meeting in New York where that was determined," Mike Brown said. "Pete Rozelle kept the owners there all day and all night, literally. Lamar [Hunt] was sleeping on a couch in the hallway. Pete just pushed them to exhaustion, and, finally,

Cleveland, Pittsburgh, and Baltimore agreed to come over and were paid something to do it.

"I think the fact the leagues became one was best for everybody. I doubt anybody today would argue otherwise."

Paul Brown had thrown his imposing weight around to help solidify realignment. And when Baltimore, Pittsburgh, and Cleveland—ah, Cleveland!—shifted to the AFC, it heightened the potential for intense rivalries.

Plus just a bit of revenge.

That vengeance would come in the very first meeting between the team Paul Brown created in Cincinnati and the one named after him in Cleveland.

"The first time we beat them, it was an exhibition in 1970, right before the first interleague games," Johnson recalled of an August 29 encounter in the second pro football game at Riverfront Stadium. "We won 31–24. I was the captain, and we had this policy of the captains giving out the game balls. We gave it to Coach Brown . . . and you could see he was as choked up as Coach Brown gets.

"What happened in Cleveland was a deep wound to a proud person. The players weren't buying what he was saying that it was just another game, or whatever Coach Brown said. It meant a lot to him."

Just as Paul Brown meant so much to the AFL.

LOU RYMKUS AND WALLY LEMM

When AFL teams were trolling for coaching candidates in 1960, they fished through the fertile waters of NFL assistants. One of the best catches was made by the Houston Oilers.

Two, actually: Lou Rymkus and Wally Lemm.

Rymkus was a rugged offensive tackle at Notre Dame and then in the NFL for the Cleveland Browns. By the end of the 1950s, he was ensconced as an assistant coach with the Rams, working with offensive linemen.

But he had a falling out with Rams coach Sid Gillman in 1959 and was eager to listen to those upstarts in the debuting AFL.

The Oilers were the most convincing talkers. In return for their faith, Rymkus guided the Oilers to the very first AFL title in the 1960 season.

And when things fell apart early in the next season, Lemm, the secondary coach the previous year, returned to replace Rymkus. All Lemm did was lead Houston to yet another crown in 1961 and then into the AFL championship game in 1962.

Rymkus and Lemm could not have been more different. Rymkus was gruff, worked his players to exhaustion at times, and had tunnel vision: football pretty much was his entire life. He once told his players, "If I'm ever standing at midfield and have a heart attack, don't let me die there. Drag my body into the end zone."

He also was the hardest worker on any coaching staff, just as he was the most diligent player on every team for which he played. And if the workload, including live scrimmages, bothered teammates or the men he coached, well, tough.

"That guy would drive you nuts," star rookie running back Billy Cannon said. "I never scrimmaged as much in my life as I did under him."

And, please, no chuckles.

"If you smiled, it was like you had committed a crime," quarterback Jacky Lee said. "If a guy laughed, Lou would stop practice and lecture us on being hard nosed. You don't get that way from lectures. You either are or you aren't. As far as I'm concerned, I think better and learn things quicker when I'm relaxed. I think most players do."

Which is how Lemm approached the game. Lemm had many outside interests, was soft spoken, and recognized the need for football to be fun.

"Pro football players, like anybody else, do their jobs better when they like their work," he said.

The early Oilers did their jobs extremely well, whether it was under the martinet Rymkus or the more subtle Lemm. With NFL veteran George Blanda engineering the prolific offense that included Cannon at halfback and brilliant receiver Charlie Hennigan, the Oilers scored 379 points in 1960. The defense featured linebacker Mike Dukes, tackle Orville Trask, and cornerback Julian Spence as Houston went 10–4 to win the Eastern Division.

Rymkus won AFL coach of the year honors, which he celebrated by ordering several thousand drinking glasses engraved with his likeness, glasses that he gave away.

Hardly the inspirational type, Rymkus simply relied on work ethic to succeed. He expected the same from his players, although he sometimes had a strange way of articulating it.

He once told his team, "Be like the great northern buffalo, whose coat is shaggy and whose muscles are strong. The great northern buffalo sticks his head into the wind and braves the cold, not like the puny southern buffalo, who turns his back to the storm."

The storm at the end of the season blew into Houston's Jeppesen Stadium from the West Coast: the Chargers, in their lone season representing Los Angeles, won the Western Division, also at 10–4 and also with a powerhouse offense. And with Gillman as their coach.

While both men tried to be cordial, there was a decided air of enmity between the coaches and their squads. It carried into the game.

"It was pretty clear that he and Gillman had no love lost for each other," Spence once said. "Basically, they wanted their team to beat the brains out of the other team, on the scoreboard and in the trenches."

Houston did most of the beating, winning 24–16. Rymkus's hard-nosed coaching techniques had worked.

Not that it earned him or his players a championship ring for their fingers, at least not immediately. Owner Bud Adams didn't bother with the baubles until years later, and when he did, according to Rymkus's son, they were sterling silver, not gold.

Rymkus was the gold standard among AFL coaches for one season and not much longer. The Oilers started out 1–3–1, and Adams impetuously dumped Rymkus, choosing a polar opposite in Lemm to take over.

According to *Sports Illustrated*, Lemm, who left Houston after the 1960 championship season, was involved in a sporting goods business back home in Libertyville, Illinois, when he was summoned by Adams. He dumped the delivery of merchandise on his wife and, with little knowledge of the 1961 team—not that it had changed much—headed to Texas.

"I had seen the team only twice, on television," Lemm told the magazine. "My general impression was that they were not hustling and that the defense was not nearly diversified enough. When I got here, I made no personnel changes for the first two weeks. I looked at a couple of game movies to find out about the players I hadn't seen before, and that first week I put in more defenses."

He also energized the Oilers. In their first game under Lemm, they faced the Dallas Texans, who had pasted them for 398 yards rushing three weeks earlier. Lemm installed a variety of defensive schemes, albeit simplified ones, and Dallas managed a mere 126 yards on the ground. Result: the Oilers routed the Texans 38–7.

And the Oilers were headed in the right direction.

The record wasn't the only reason Rymkus was fired. Adams felt that Rymkus had too little patience with rookies, noting that Houston signed eight of its first 11 draft picks despite competition from the NFL. But Rymkus rarely gave the kids a chance.

"I guess the thing that really frosted me was Lou's insistence on keeping Charlie Milstead at safety," Adams told *Sports Illustrated*. "I'm no football expert, but in the first game we lost, against San Diego, the Chargers ate Milstead up. I didn't say anything. Then the Texans beat us, and they took advantage of Milstead, too.

"I asked Lou about it after that game. We had a good defensive back named Fred Glick sitting on the bench. Lou said he'd try him. Then we played Buffalo, and Milstead went all the way again, and we got beat again. I talked to Lou some more about it, and he said Glick was ready now and he'd use him against Boston. We should have won that game, but Milstead went all the way again, and they tied us 31–31."

Bye-bye, Lou.

Hello, Wally.

Before Lemm took the job, though, he said he had major concerns.

"I worried about it for three days before accepting, but some coaching friends of mine told me I'd be crazy to turn down the opportunity. The first couple of weeks I was here, I worked so hard, I didn't begin to worry until Friday."

Not to worry—nobody was taking down Lemm's Oilers.

The Oilers won their last seven regular-season contests under Lemm as the defense remained staunch and the offense took flight behind Blanda, one of 14 all-stars and the league's most valuable player.

En route to the title game, Lemm won the AFL's coach-of-the-year honors.

This time, the title game was at San Diego. Lemm had no feuds going with Gillman, just a healthy respect for one of football's most innovative minds.

Oh, yeah, Lemm also had some defensive twists for Chargers quarterback Jack Kemp.

"They had us guessing all game," Kemp said. "You'd expect them to come from one place, and they came from another. Or they sent more guys than we could block, and we couldn't get the ball out.

"Coach Lemm really had them prepared for us."

Indeed, the Oilers sacked Kemp six times, held the Chargers to a measly field goal, and won their second straight championship. Final: Houston 10, San Diego 3.

It was one for Lou and one for Wally.

Neither would coach a team to another championship.

MIKE HOLOVAK

"Stability" was not a buzzword for the Boston Patriots, who traipsed all around Beantown like homeless children looking for a warm fireplace and a friendly family to take them in. While they searched for a place to call home, hosting games in four stadiums, the Patriots managed some order on the sideline.

Although Mike Holovak was not the team's initial head coach—Saban, of course, was in charge for one season and eventually coached two other AFL franchises—Holovak lasted seven seasons leading the Patriots. Until Bill Belichick, that was the longest coaching run for anyone in New England.

"Mike was a mentor, a coach, a friend, and, above all, a consummate gentleman," said Gino Cappelletti, one of the Patriots' early greats. "His contributions as coach and general manager in the critical early years of the Patriots' franchise were monumental."

Holovak began his tenure with the Patriots as director of player personnel and offensive backfield coach. He already had been a success as a player and coach at Boston College and eventually would prove himself as a scout, general manager, and executive, along with his coaching prowess.

That success probably stemmed from the dearth of talent at Boston College, where Holovak often juggled players' positions. Weekly.

"Mike was the quintessential 'football guy,'" original Houston Oilers owner Bud Adams said. "It is rare when you see a person excel in all three areas of the sport—a great player in college, a successful coach, and great talent evaluator—but Mike was one of the special people."

The Patriots were anything but special in their initial campaign, going 5–9 under Saban, losing their last four games. When they began the 1961 season 2–3, Saban was out, Holovak in.

And the Pats were in good shape, going 7–1–1 the rest of the way under the low-key Holovak.

As Boston sportswriter Will McDonough once wrote, "Billy Sullivan founded the Patriots, but the guy who saved them was Holovak. It was his personality and the love his players had for him that kept the team afloat in its first decade of existence. The team won consistently with the lowest payroll in the league and the worst practice conditions imaginable."

Those conditions included the lack of a true home, whether for practice or for games. The Patriots also struggled when the AFL–NFL bidding wars for players began because the Sullivan family always seemed to be cutting corners financially.

But Holovak made it work by understanding the franchise's limitations.

"We concentrate on smaller areas," Holovak said of the scouting approach. "When the two leagues were competing, we felt we'd have little chance to sign a boy from the Far West, for example, if the Rams or 49ers had drafted the same boy. Then, too, we can learn more about players from our own area because we can scout them more frequently."

By 1962, Boston was an Eastern Division contender, and in 1963, the Patriots made the playoffs for the first time, winning at Buffalo to get to the AFL title game.

"If I have any secret," Holovak said, "it's that we work hard and this team is gifted with fellows who stick together and believe in themselves. We can play anybody to a standstill, and we know it."

Almost anybody: The Chargers routed the Patriots 51–10 in the championship game.

One noteworthy statistic in Holovak's résumé was his 5–27 record in preseason games. Holovak treated those contests exactly as they should be—as exhibitions and the season's preparations. Jon Morris, the Patriots' all-decade center for the 1960s, joined the team in 1964, and that approach was immediately noticeable.

"I came in from the College All-Star Game, so I was late getting to training camp, and the exhibition season was starting as soon as I got there," Morris said. "And we proceeded to lose every one of our exhibition games. We looked terrible. And Mike made no effort to win the games.

"After the last one, I'm walking off the field, and Babe [Parilli] says to me, 'Don't you worry about this. This is how we do it every season. We never take the exhibition games seriously. We'll be ready to go when it starts.'

"He was right. We had a great season. We ended up winning our first four games. I thought, 'Well, you have to listen to the veterans. They know what they're talking about.'"

When the Patriots slipped to 3–10–1 and 4–10 marks in 1967 and 1968, Holovak lost his coaching position to Clive Rush. Holovak continued to work in pro football in a variety of positions for several teams until retiring in 1999.

Jack Kemp, one of the AFL's best quarterbacks with San Diego and Buffalo, praised Holovak's coaching work. Kemp said that Holovak's teams were always among the best prepared.

"You have to give credit to the guy on the sideline making the decisions, the Gillmans and Strams and Holovaks."

Nice company to keep.

GEORGE WILSON

Ranking George Wilson with the best and brightest sideline bosses of the AFL is a stretch.

Rating him among the great characters who coached in the AFL? A sure thing.

Wilson's numbers from the NFL were quite decent: 53–45–6 with the Lions, guiding Detroit to its last championship in 1957. He left the Lions in 1964 and was hired as the Miami Dolphins' first head coach for their 1966 expansion season.

Working with a raggedy bunch that either couldn't score or couldn't stop anybody—or both—Wilson went 15–39–2 in four seasons at the Dolphins' helm. Perhaps his main claim to fame in Miami was preceding Don Shula.

But Wilson's players have some vivid memories of him.

"George was old-school football," says original Dolphins guard Norm Evans. "I remember after a game we lost at San Diego, George got up on a table in the locker room and was furious because they left their first team in for most of the exhibition game. So George screams at us, 'I'll tell you what, our coaching staff can whip their coaching staff.'"

There wasn't much whipping going on by the Dolphins in those early days, never coming close to a winning record. The Dolphins lost their first five games before finally getting a victory, beating Denver 24–7 at home, then winning at Houston 20–13. But from day 1, they were getting whipped into shape by Wilson, who didn't have much use for the sun and fun that South Florida always offers.

"These outside attractions—the swimming pools, the beach, and fancy living—won't have much appeal to my guys once we get through working them," Wilson said at his first training camp. "They'll value the rest much more.

"Don't look for any of my players running around with golf clubs on their backs. They won't feel like golf. If they do, I won't have done my job on the practice field."

The practice fields were, well, a bit crowded in the early days of the Dolphins. So much so that Wilson and his staff sometimes needed to send marginal players home just so they could find time to look at the true prospects.

"There wasn't much room for players here," Wilson said. "We knew we were going to use 40 when the season opened, and we had something like 125 to look at. I've had to cut boys and watch tears flow until it hurt me.

"But I've also tried to tell each one of them whether to continue in this game or to try some other profession. I appreciate the problems of the players. If I can help them, I try to. I like to think I am more than a coach to my boys."

He was more than a coach to one of the quarterbacks, a fellow named George Wilson Jr. The younger Wilson had never started a game in college at Xavier, a top basketball school in Cincinnati with a small-time football program. With the Dolphins, the coach's son replaced Rick Norton after the first-round draft pick struggled mightily during the early losing streak.

Nepotism? A little, sure, because Wilson Jr. was not drafted and probably wouldn't have stuck with any other pro teams.

An enlightened decision? You bet, as the youngster led Miami to its first two victories.

Initially asked if George Jr. was tough enough to make the Dolphins, his father replied, "He sure better be. If not, I'll make him tougher."

And after the dad put the son in the lineup and he succeeded, Wilson Sr. added, "Nobody should be surprised at George Jr. He has been going to training camp since he was seven years old. He learned how to punt from Yale Lary and how to pass from Bobby Layne."

Wilson Jr. would not go on to a Hall of Fame career. In fact, he lasted only that one season with the Dolphins.

His dad made it through four, the subject of colorful stories along the way.

Try this one: "We were in New England, and they said it was 38 degrees and it had been pouring rain there for two weeks," Evans recalls. "Rick Norton was our starting quarterback, and I remember [Larry] Csonka was there. The field at Boston College's stadium was just a puddle. On the whole sideline the water was up to your ankles. There had been a game there the day before, so it was a quagmire, and it was so cold. Everybody was soaked to the bone.

"Early in the game, our quarterback got so cold he had hypothermia, and he was shaking so hard he couldn't call the plays. So Wilson sent the trainer back to the locker room to get his briefcase, and George pulls out a fifth of whiskey from it. He gives Rick a big jolt of it to catch his breath. And whatever it does, it warmed him up.

"Then everybody wanted some, but nobody had the guts to ask."

5

A TV Sport

Without television, pro football never would have become America's sport. Way back in the early 1960s, Pete Rozelle realized that the quickest (and most lucrative) path to respect, recognition, and even reverence was through the tube.

As Rozelle cut profitable deals with the networks back then, setting in motion the spiraling rights fees that eventually would dwarf everything in TV sports, the AFL wasn't sitting by in envious invisibility. The "little league that could" was getting its games on national television, too.

In the end, TV money lifted the AFL higher than one of Joe Namath's soaring passes to Don Maynard.

"Of course TV saved the league," said Len Dawson, whose Chiefs would become one of the most popular AFL clubs thanks to the national exposure provided by ABC and then NBC.

It wasn't just Dawson's team that benefited.

"The ABC contract right off the bat helped with the exposure, and it was very important to the success of the AFL," said original Chargers owner Barron Hilton. "And in 1965, when NBC got the rights, that gave every club sufficient funds to where they could be all profitable from that point on. We were all elated to get NBC."

Before the AFL could get anywhere with NBC, though, it did business with ABC.

Back when the "Foolish Club" was putting together its not-so-foolish plans, pro football on television was something of a free-for-all. Right up until the AFL's first kickoff, some of the established teams in the NFL had their own deals—and own TV networks.

In 1960, when the eight AFL franchises opened for business, 11 of the 13 NFL clubs were affiliated with CBS. The Baltimore Colts and Pittsburgh Steelers had tie-ins with NBC, the first time that network did regular-season NFL contests. And NBC had rights to the NFL title game.

Where did that leave the AFL?

"There were two options, really," Chiefs owner Lamar Hunt said. "Each franchise could form its own regional network or just be televised locally. Or the whole league could go national."

Had Rozelle been in the mood to advise these upstarts, he would have suggested—no, insisted—that they go the national route. Fortunately, Hunt, Hilton, Buffalo owner Ralph Wilson, and the other league founders were on the same wavelength as the NFL commissioner.

But where could these newcomers sell their wares? That was as simple as ABC.

Considered the third network back then, ABC grabbed the opportunity to get into the sport. It would be more than a decade before ABC would become synonymous with pro football—the college brand was its staple—but the broadcasts guaranteed the AFL key financial footing with a five-year series of contracts.

ABC added a twist, too. While it would black out games in home markets, it would instead show out-of-town contests, ensuring that every AFL market would have a televised game each Sunday.

"We had a five-year deal with ABC, a series of five one-year deals that was renewable each year," Hunt explained. "The first year, I think we got $100,000 per team. The second year it went down because sales were not as good."

While each NFL team had its own play-by-play man—Ray Scott for Green Bay, for example, and Jack Whitaker for Philadelphia—ABC (and later NBC) was not so parochial. And though Jack Buck years later would become among the most recognizable of NFL voices, he handled AFL play-by-play duties in 1960 and 1961, including the first two title games.

One of the most lasting and identifiable of the AFL announcers was Charlie Jones, and he was there from the very beginning.

"I did the first AFL game ever televised in 1960," he said. "It was between the Dallas Texans and the Los Angeles Chargers at the Coliseum, and I remember two things about it.

"First, they listed the attendance at 19,000, but you sure couldn't find them. And two, my producer was a guy named Roone Arledge, who went on to slightly bigger things with ABC."

Before Arledge invented *Monday Night Football* in 1970, however, he was just another guy giving out directions on the game set.

Jones, though, became a familiar figure to AFL fans right away. It stayed that way throughout the league's life span.

"As a kid growing up [in the New York area], what I identify with the early AFL and the Jets and the Titans was Charlie," said Bob Parente, who became the Jets' vice president of broadcasting and production. "Certainly for any of our fans in the sixties, he was the guy."

Actually, Jones never was *the guy* at ABC or NBC, with Buck and then Curt Gowdy getting the most prestigious assignments. But Jones became the unofficial verbal wordsmith of the AFL because those announcers—and many others who did pro football—also were readily identified with other sports (Buck with baseball's St. Louis Cardinals, Gowdy with the Red Sox and *American Sportsman*).

"Charlie was a consummate professional, always one of the most prepared announcers, and a really good guy," longtime Jets publicist Frank Ramos said. "It was very good for the AFL to have a guy who cared as much about the league as he did."

Although TV ratings weren't particularly high for the AFL on ABC in the first two seasons, the 1962 and 1963 championship games would be watershed events that would bring exactly the kind of acclaim team owners sought.

The 1962 title matchup between Dallas and Houston went into double overtime, the longest game in pro football history at that point. Played on December 23, one week before the NFL's ultimate game, the Texans' thrilling 20–17 victory caught the attention of the sporting public. The game had everything, including a second half marred by a wicked storm known as a "Blue Norther."

"It was a newsworthy event, a longer game than any other in pro football, and it was an AFL championship game," Hunt said. "It was very memorable, and a lot of people saw it."

A year later, when San Diego's powerhouse routed the Patriots in the championship contest, again as the only game of the day, interest in the AFL was unprecedented.

Recalled Al Locasale, who served as a scout, administrator, and executive with the Chargers, Raiders, and Bengals, "The 1963 championship game where we beat Boston 51–10 was on TV, and it did not have direct competition from an NFL game. So people watched that game because they wanted to see football, and it had a vast audience of people who did not have familiarity with the AFL. I was out the next week, and people were saying to me, 'You guys have great players, that was a hell of a football team.'

"That telecast created a tremendous amount of visibility and memorability."

It also piqued interest at NBC, which was eager to get a bigger share of the pro football pie.

With interest in the NFL surging, Rozelle found himself in an unprecedented position of power. CBS's two-year contract had expired, and both NBC and ABC eagerly joined the bidding for the next deal. Rozelle insisted on sealed bids.

ABC was so interested in claiming NFL rights that it doubled the previous CBS rights fee of $9.3 million for two years.

Rozelle then opened the NBC bid, which was for triple what the league previously received.

But CBS, considered the top network because of its collection of stars in news (Edward R. Murrow and Walter Cronkite) and entertainment (Dick Van Dyke, Lucille Ball, and anyone who appeared on Ed Sullivan's show), wasn't about to take a backseat in sports. Rozelle already had earned his league unimagined riches, and even he was astonished when he pulled out the CBS bid: $28.2 million for two years.

"That was huge money, the biggest ever in sports," Hunt noted.

Then the AFL owners pounced on the fact NBC had money to spend and no place to spend it. The "Peacock Network" found the place to spend it very quickly.

The AFL's lead man in the negotiations was Sonny Werblin, who bought the Titans in 1963, renamed them the Jets, and would soon change the sports landscape with his momentous signing of Joe Namath. First, Werblin, a well-known show business entrepreneur who had been with MCA television when it negotiated the ABC contract for the AFL, made a huge impact by rapidly closing a deal with NBC.

The value: $36 million over five years. Each of the eight AFL franchises would get $850,000 a year.

"We were at a banquet at the Garden City Hotel," Ramos remembered, "and Howard Cosell was the emcee. Sonny came over and told me about the deal, and he said that it gave the AFL the money with which they could go and compete for players.

"That really put the AFL on solid ground. The owners knew they could go out and sign players."

So much money also changed the perception of the AFL throughout America—inside football and outside.

"There was a lot of negative media," Chiefs executive Jack Steadman said. "You know, the AFL is going to collapse every year. And we didn't get the coverage that the NFL was getting.

"The big change was when we got our new television contract with NBC. That gave all the teams resources that we really needed to compete for players. And at that point, the NFL saw that they were in a war with people that could stay in the war. So things started to change dramatically during the 1964 season. Then early in '65, we became pretty good with strong teams. We were signing some top players against the NFL."

Suddenly, the NFL's view of these AFL interlopers changed, too.

"Our owners realized they were not going away when NBC signed them to a new, big-money contract," said NFL official Joe Browne, Rozelle's and successor Paul Tagliabue's right-hand man. "They had economic stability with that TV money."

NBC in those days also was considered much more of a showcase network than was ABC. With such staples as The *Today* show and the *Tonight* show, plus stars Milton Berle, Jack Paar, and, later, Johnny Carson and premier newsmen such as Chet Huntley and David Brinkley, America paid attention to NBC.

And now it might just pay attention to the American Football League.

The recently married Hunt was on his honeymoon in Europe when he was told about what some were calling the AFL's "lifeblood." From the Winter Olympics in Innsbruck, Austria, he and Wilson, who also was at the Games, made a rather expensive telephone call back to the States to get details of the contract Werblin had negotiated.

"It was a dramatic increase," Hunt said. "We were surprised. It was important in keeping the venture alive."

Important? It was essential.

"Nobody need be hit on the head with a goalpost to be brought to the realization that $36 million is a rather staggering figure," wrote Carl Lindemann, NBC's vice president for sports, in the AFL's 1965 media guide. "It is, in fact, the largest sum ever paid in a sports television contract.

"One doesn't enter a contract of this magnitude without knowing something about the other party involved. We knew the men operating the AFL franchises were men of financial means."

NBC brought something new to pro football, televising some games in 1965 "in living color." By the next season, colorized telecasts were the norm.

And what NBC was showing was captivating to viewers: the aerial strikes of San Diego's John Hadl to Lance Alworth, the head-hunting defenders in Oakland, and Boston's brilliantly versatile Gino Cappelletti, a wide receiver and placekicker extraordinaire, as well as playmaking defensive backs in Kansas City (Johnny Robinson) and Oakland (Dave Grayson), ball-hunting linebackers (Bobby Bell, Nick Buoniconti, and Larry Grantham), and tackle-breaking runners (Jim Nance, Matt Snell, and Clem Daniels) and the men who cleared their paths (Billy Shaw, Ron Mix, and Jim Otto).

The guys in the booth were pretty accomplished, too. Gowdy and Jones became the most recognizable voices of the AFL. Both were flexible enough to handle a variety of sports—indeed, Gowdy was better known for baseball and basketball coverage for much of his career.

"He was the first superstar of sports television because he did all of the big events," colleague Dick Enberg said of Gowdy. "He's the last of the dinosaurs. No one will ever be the voice of so many major events at the same time ever again."

Gowdy landed one particular plum, the first Super Bowl telecast, on which Jones worked the sidelines. Gowdy also became involved in another classic, the *Heidi* game, which might be even more famous than the first AFL–NFL championship. It's certainly more infamous in TV annals.

And he called Super Bowl III, considered the most significant game of the Super Bowl era.

In fact, Gowdy and Paul Christman always did the AFL's biggest contests, including its title games for ABC from 1962 to 1964, then for NBC through the remainder of the league's existence.

LANCE ALWORTH

His nickname was Bambi, and not necessarily for the reasons you might think.

Sure, Lance Alworth ran with the grace of a deer or a gazelle. And he certainly was just as elusive.

But the Hall of Fame receiver got his moniker only in part for his playing style.

"My first day in training camp in San Diego," Alworth recalled, "Charlie Flowers, who was a fullback at Ole Miss, saw me after practice when I walked in, and I had a flat-top haircut and big brown eyes. And I lifted my knees high when I ran. He said something about all that and, 'You run like a deer, and we're going to call you Bambi.' And it stuck.

"They began calling me that, then they started shortening it to Bam. Later on in my career, I could hear the younger guys whispering, 'Hey, there goes Mr. Alworth.' They were not even calling me Bambi."

That didn't bother Alworth at all.

"I am glad just it's out there," he added with a laugh, "because it's one of the few [nicknames] we can talk about."

What everyone can talk about, loudly and clearly, is Alworth's great performances and his impact on the sport. The first AFL player elected to the Pro Football Hall of Fame (in 1978), he caught 542 passes for 10,266 yards in 11 seasons, an 18.94-yard average, and scored 85 touchdowns.

During his nine seasons with the Chargers, he averaged more than 50 catches and 1,000 yards per year. He caught a pass in every AFL game in which he participated, 105, including all-star games; Alworth made seven straight all-league teams from 1963 to 1969.

But he never even thought about a pro football career before attending the University of Arkansas or even while he was having an all-America career with the Razorbacks.

"You have to go back to those years and in 1961–63, remember that pro football was just becoming really popular and had not hit the popularity where it is today," he said. "I played in the South, and there were no pro teams in the South at the time. I can remember the Colts winning the championship game, and my dad was watching it, and I didn't even watch it. It was not something everyone paid attention to in those days. You didn't think about it when playing in high school or college, that you could go to pro ball.

"When I was at Arkansas, they held the early draft for us, and Lamar Hunt and the Texans said they were going to draft me."

The only problem: the Texans wanted Alworth to play defensive back, something he didn't want to do.

"So I told the Texans, 'Don't waste your time, I am not interested in defensive back, I'll go to law school.'"

Alworth was a running back in college, but Al Davis was convinced that Alworth would make a superb wideout. Davis was the receivers coach at San Diego. He knew that his boss at the time, Chargers coach Sid Gillman, would make the adjustment work.

"I didn't know if I could play at receiver," Alworth said.

That didn't stop Davis from recruiting Alworth. Talk about working a room.

"He met all my family and my wife's family at the time and everybody loved him," Alworth recalled. "They still do. In the 1980s, he was still calling my parents, and I was not even playing. He'd even be calling from the airplane: 'This is your favorite football coach.'

"Al used to watch us warm up at Arkansas, where we almost always ran the ball. Al asked me about becoming a receiver, and I said, 'Yeah, I love to catch the football.'

"He said, 'Well, I thought you did, and the only time I get to see you catch the football is in warm-ups.'"

Davis was the main reason that Alworth wound up with the Chargers. He had also been drafted by the NFL's San Francisco 49ers, but that didn't work out for one special reason.

"I met with their coach Red Hickey in a Jackson, Mississippi, hotel, and he said are you interested in playing? And what do you want?

"I told him first of all, the AFL offered me a no-cut contract for two years. And he said, 'We will never give no-cut contracts.'

"So I said, 'Well, you know, it has been nice meeting you,' and I walked out the door and never spoke to them again. I was drafted number 1 by them, and that was the last time they got in touch with me."

The 49ers' loss was not only the Chargers' gain but also the AFL's. No team epitomized the downfield, bombs-away style that is often remembered more than San Diego.

"I believe that was the beginning of the West Coast offense, what we had in San Diego," Alworth said. "Sid was the inventor of it, he started it all. He had an innovative way of looking at it, and once he put the system together and John [Hadl] learned how to run it, we knew we could score points. It was fun to play, it was totally different than anything I had played in college.

"I loved to catch the football and run with it, and this gave me the opportunity to do what I did best and enjoyed the most."

Alworth seemed fated to be in the right place and time for his unique talents.

"That was the perfect place for me to play and for John to play," he said. "But we had no idea beforehand or even in that period of time how influential that offense would be."

"It was exciting to grow with the AFL during that period," Gowdy said.

For Super Bowl I, NBC shared the job with CBS. Two networks handling one game? You bet.

While that was a coup for the leagues, it made for some strange bedfellows on the broadcast side. Because neither NBC nor CBS was willing to forgo televising the historic first meeting between the league champions, Rozelle was plenty content to let them both have their way. CBS provided the video feed.

Gowdy might have been too hyped up for the game. Early on, he said, "And here come the captains, out for the *toin coss.*"

Neither network particularly distinguished itself during Green Bay's 35–10 victory over Kansas City. The broadcasts were solid, if a bit tinged with favoritism for the league each one covered.

NBC did put one over on CBS when game producer Ted Nathanson brought a large TV set into the production truck. He trained a camera on the screen, then would zoom in to show a tighter shot to the viewers at home. CBS's crew had no idea where NBC was getting such exclusive shots.

While Christman and later Kyle Rote and Al DeRogatis were terrific analysts, Gowdy was the star of the show for the AFL—as synonymous with the league as Vin Scully became with the Dodgers or Bud Collins with Wimbledon.

"When you heard Curt Gowdy on a football game or a baseball game, it didn't matter who was playing; it was like listening to the Super Bowl or the World Series," said former ABC executive Dennis Lewin. "You knew it was a big event because Curt Gowdy was there."

One of Gowdy's most memorable broadcasts occurred on November 17, 1968: New York Jets versus the Oakland Raiders. The Jets–Raiders series had turned into one of the AFL's most fierce and into one of the ugliest rivalries in pro sports, so it was a spotlight matchup.

Little did anyone know that the spotlight would be stolen by a little girl from the Alps. Scotty Connal, NBC's executive producer of sports, might have been the most surprised.

Connal had come to work that day without a clue that he would be at the center of one of the worst firestorms in sports broadcasting history.

All he was thinking about was making sure the Jets–Raiders game got on the air without a hitch. If things went smoothly, which they normally did, the game would be over in time to broadcast the scheduled showing of the children's movie classic *Heidi* at 7:00 p.m. Eastern Time.

Connal settled back to watch a superb game featuring the passing of Namath and Daryle Lamonica. It was an exciting, close battle with lots of points, which meant lots of stoppages.

"It was becoming a terribly slow fourth quarter," Connal said. "I was a little nervous."

Would the game be over in time to broadcast *Heidi*? That was Connal's only worry.

The Jets' fans were worried, too, but for another reason. They feared that their team would blow the lead it held: 32–29 with less than a minute left when NBC cut to a commercial.

Before that break, Connal had been in touch with NBC Sports head Carl Lindemann. Connal wanted to know if he should discontinue the showing of the game and switch to *Heidi* at 7:00 p.m., as planned.

Lindemann got on the phone with NBC president Julian Goodman.

"What about the instruction to broadcast operations control that *Heidi* had to go on promptly at 7:00 p.m. ET, no matter what?" Lindemann asked.

"That's crazy," Goodman said. "It's a terrible idea."

Terrible, indeed. He had no idea how terrible. What followed was a series of frantic phone calls, missed connections, and misunderstandings that would have done justice to any Hollywood screwball comedy. Phone calls bounced from coast to coast in a crazy-quilt pattern in an attempt to straighten things out.

Connal was instructed: keep the game on to its conclusion, forget about *Heidi* for the moment.

Connal called New York to relay that order but was unable to get through.

Frantic, Connal called the production truck at the Oakland Coliseum. He told the producer to call the NBC studios in Burbank, California, to emphasize that the Jets–Raiders game should stay on the air. Operators in Burbank were to relay that message to New York.

With the game in a commercial break, the board operator in New York, Don Cline, received word from Burbank. Because it contradicted his orders that *Heidi* must hit the air at 7:00 p.m. sharp, Cline opted to call Connal for confirmation.

All Cline got was a busy signal; Connal was still on his two phone lines, one with the truck in Oakland and one with Lindemann.

Where was a cell phone when you needed one? Obviously, far into the future.

So Cline followed his original orders.

"I waited and waited and heard nothing," Cline said. "We came up to that magic hour and I thought, 'Well, I haven't been given any [confirmation of the] counterorder, so I've got to do what we agreed to do.'"

And he did, setting off a broadcast blaze. At the bewitching hour of 7:00 p.m., *Heidi* went on the air, leaving Raiders, Jets, and their fans completely in the dark.

The switchboard at the NBC studios in New York lit up like the Christmas tree at Rockefeller Center as angry football fans voiced

GEORGE SAIMES

George Saimes was a standout safety for Buffalo from 1963 to 1969, helping the Bills win two championships. He finished his playing career with the Denver Broncos in 1972 before going into scouting for Tampa, Washington, and Houston. He remained in the scouting profession for more than 30 years. Saimes was selected to the AFL all-time team.

As an all-American at Michigan State, I was drafted by both the AFL and NFL. The Dallas Texans had my rights and eventually traded them to the Bills. The Los Angeles Rams had my rights in the NFL.

Both teams were offering the same amount of money. Dick McCann, the director of the Pro Football Hall of Fame, advised me to try to get a little more bonus money. Also have it in my contract that I'll get half my salary when I report to camp. He was a little worried whether I was going to make it or not. I was only 5-foot-11, 186 pounds.

I followed his advice and asked Bills owner Ralph Wilson for the extra money. I doubled the bonus and got the salary money I wanted.

I'll tell you a funny story about the equipment I used with the Bills:

My senior year, I had gone to New York to pick up my all-American award. There was a writer from my home town that covered the Cleveland Browns. They were playing the Giants, and I went to their pregame practice. And then I went to the game, too. I was in the locker room, and I was introduced to Lou Groza, the great Browns' kicker. And I was sitting there, and at that time, I didn't realize it, Lou wasn't playing much, he was just kicking.

I looked down at his helmet; it was sitting on the floor. It was one of these old-fashioned suspension helmets with only two straps, crisscrossed.

I looked at it and said, "Lou, you wear that helmet?" Groza said, "Yeah, what's wrong with it?" At that time, they had come in with a better suspension system inside the helmet . . . several straps, all the way around.

I thought, *My God, the Cleveland Browns are still using those old suspension helmets!* The old helmets scared me to death.

Well, when I joined the Bills, I took all my equipment from college with me—any kind of pads I had, shoulder pads, thigh pads, knee pads, foot pads. I took them with me to Buffalo because I didn't know what kind of equipment they had.

Turns out, I later realized Groza was just kicking, so he had the old suspension helmet. It was funny. I wore my shoulder pads from college the first five or six years. They kept telling me to get them replaced. They sent them to reconditioning every year because the one side was always caved in, and finally I replaced them after so many years.

I don't think anyone realizes how great a defensive team we had in Buffalo. I didn't realize it myself until after all those years. You don't realize how good the defense is until after you start looking at that stuff. I don't know if it's any indication of how good we were, but when they picked the fiftieth anniversary team, four of us made it. And, you know, they had some really good players in the nineties when they went to four Super Bowls. For people to vote four guys from the sixties onto that team was amazing.

There was Tom Sestak, Mike Stratton, myself, and Butch Byrd. That said a lot for our defense. We had a really good defensive coordinator at that time, Joel Collier.

When I retired, I stayed in the game as a scout, something like 32 years. The NFL has been good to me. I was playing, and I was lucky I came out healthy.

their complaints. The switchboard couldn't handle the load and blew out.

"I didn't do anything wrong," Cline later said defensively. "I'm not guilty here. I did what I was supposed to do. In fact, NBC promoted me the following month."

Back home in suburban New York City, Goodman expected NBC to come back to Oakland, not go to the mountains of Austria.

"Where in hell has our football game gone?" Goodman roared to Lindemann over the phone.

Lindemann was trying to placate Goodman and at the same time shouting to Connal through another phone that his wife was holding.

He grabbed the phone out of his wife's hand and repeated Goodman's question: "Where in hell has our football game gone?"

Connal was momentarily silent. Then, he was ready to cry.

"Oakland has scored a touchdown," he told Lindemann.

Not one, but two.

"While I am still trying to explain to Goodman about that touchdown," said Lindemann, "I hear Scotty shouting in my other ear, 'My God, Oakland has scored another touchdown!'"

The Raiders won 43–32. Gowdy might have been at his most evocative calling those final frantic moments, but most of the country wouldn't have known it.

"I didn't know we were off the air," Gowdy told the *St. Louis Post-Dispatch*. "When the game was over, I was packing to get out of there, and the stage manager yelled at me, 'Hey, you've got to do those two touchdowns again!'"

Gowdy might have replied, "There's no do-overs in football," but the idea was that NBC would replay the final moments of what was now an AFL classic on Monday morning's *Today* show.

Always a pro, Gowdy recreated the crazy final minutes.

Not long after Oakland's sensational yet invisible comeback, Goodman apologized publicly.

"The most significant factor to come out of *Heidi* was, whatever you do, you better not leave an NFL football game," said Val Pinchbeck, the NFL's senior vice president of broadcasting. "Ten years earlier, if you did the same thing on a telecast, would you get the same type of uproar? I don't know. But you sure did at that point in time."

Gowdy and Christman would be at the microphones six weeks later when the Jets did hold on, beating the Raiders 27–23 to earn a berth in Super Bowl III. No *Heidi* this time—in fact, no problems at all.

The Jets' monumental upset of the Colts in the third Super Bowl was Gowdy's favorite assignment. After all, he'd chronicled the AFL during its early years and through the bidding wars with the NFL and then into the Super Bowl age—and through the heavy criticism of the AFL from NFL-oriented media.

"That game will always stand out as the most memorable event in my broadcast career," he said.

"I would say Super Bowl III wasn't the best game I ever broadcast or the most exciting, but it was a historic game that changed the thinking of America about the AFL. Suddenly everyone started to say they were as good as the NFL, which from top to bottom they weren't. But that really changed the outlook of pro football and was probably the greatest upset of all time."

Gowdy got some satisfaction out of it off the air. During a commercial break, when it was apparent the Jets would win, Gowdy thought about *Sports Illustrated* writer Tex Maule, perhaps the loudest critic of the upstart league. And Gowdy said, "I wonder if that son-of-a-bitch Tex Maule is watching?"

By the 1970 merger, NBC was ensconced as the AFL's network. The NFL would earn $185 million in a four-year deal with CBS, NBC, and ABC, which came aboard to televise *Monday Night Football*.

The marriage of pro football and the NFL had been consummated. There would be a divorce with NBC decades later, then a return by the network.

And there would even be rumblings that perhaps television had too strong a role in how the NFL's product was presented, too much power in deciding who played when and where.

"Most of what TV does wrong is done to generate more dollars for owners," Arledge once said. "If we cram 18 commercials into a football game it's because the owners and the leagues are so damned greedy. Sport used to be run as a hobby by owners; now it's a tax shelter for a lot of them. . . .

"Most criticism about TV and sport does not concern itself with ethics or morality."

Cameras all over the field, too many commercial breaks, unusual schedules—these are some of the common complaints against TV. Sometimes the TV God really goes over the top—as it did when NBC made the teams kick off twice at the half in the 1967 Super Bowl. The reason: the network was in commercials during the original kickoff.

"That was going a little too far," Arledge admitted.

According to Chet Simmons, who ran sports at NBC, "We really don't give 10 seconds of thought a year to how we affect sport; we're in the broadcast business."

And teams recognize TV as a necessity to stay afloat, despite any negative conditions.

"So many sports organizations have built their entire budgets around television that if we ever withdrew the money, the whole structure would just collapse," Arledge once said.

Rozelle was in unshakable agreement.

"Without our television fees, our payrolls would be half what they are," Rozelle said during his time as commissioner. "We would not be able to attract some fine college athletes. They'd be working for General Electric—and we'd be out some of the better players in our league."

6

The Greatest Game Ever, AFL Style

If the 1958 NFL championship game was considered the greatest ever played, what does that make the AFL title matchup between Dallas and Houston four years later?

All the Baltimore Colts and New York Giants did in 1958 was play a few minutes into overtime. The Texans and Oilers in 1962 went a whole overtime period longer.

Of course, neither AFL team had quite the notoriety of the Johnny Unitas/Raymond Berry/Lenny Moore Colts or the Charley Conerly/Frank Gifford/Sam Huff Giants.

The Texans didn't even have the pedigree of their Lone Star rivals, the two-time AFL champion Houston Oilers, when the AFL's third season began. The Texans were a mere .500 team through two campaigns, with nary a playoff appearance. The Oilers were the best the fledgling league had to offer.

Indeed, the Texans were still trying to erase memories of one of the worst franchises in pro sports history, the 1952 version that played in the NFL.

Those woeful Texans debuted on September 28, 1952, after Dallas millionaire Giles Miller took over what had been the New York Yankees. The Yankees went 1–9–2 the previous season, but the Texans would be even worse.

In its 1952 opener, Dallas took a 6–0 lead over the New York Giants, then was blanked the rest of the way in a 24–6 defeat. Such losses would become common, but even worse, Miller ran out of money after seven games. The league took over the franchise for the rest of its only season, a 1–11 campaign that soured Big D on the pro game for years.

"There is room in Texas for all kinds of football," Miller had claimed.

But not a football team with few assets and fewer fans. The Texans were so poorly supported in Dallas that they were forced to move one of their games out of state.

Their ignominious run included a holiday game in Akron, Ohio, against the Chicago Bears that was the second part of a Thanksgiving Day doubleheader. The stands were so empty for the Bears–Texans matchup that Texans coach Jimmy Phelan suggested sending the players "into the stands and shake hands with each fan."

Then the Texans shocked the Bears 27–23.

A few weeks later, the Dallas experiment with pro football was over.

Until Lamar Hunt came along, that is, and plunked his Texans of this newfangled American Football League into the Cotton Bowl and promoted the dickens out of the area.

Hunt was the most unpretentious of sports figures, the anti–Jerry Jones if you will. It was common to see Hunt in line at the concession stand waiting along with the fans. No special privileges just because he happened to be the owner of the team. If he got hungry at a game, he simply got up and bought himself a hotdog and a soda.

"Someone would come up to him and say, 'You look just like Lamar Hunt.' They just couldn't believe he was in a concession line," longtime business colleague Jack Steadman said.

It was easy to see why Hunt was such a beloved figure in Dallas—also because of his business acumen.

"He had great vision with a particular attention to detail," current NFL commissioner Roger Goodell said. "He realized the game was what was important, not individuals."

And Hunt rapidly built a strong organization led by coach Hank Stram and featuring quarterback Len Dawson, running back Abner Haynes, and defensive back Johnny Robinson. Dawson was the league's player of the year in 1962, when Stram was its top coach and running back Curtis McClinton its best rookie.

Still, the Texans paled in comparison to their cross-state rival in Houston. The Oilers were dynamic right from the outset, with stars aplenty (1959 Heisman Trophy winner Billy Cannon, whom the AFL stole away from the established NFL; George Blanda; Charlie Hennigan; Charley Tolar; and Bill Groman). They were an offensive machine, scoring 513 points in their second year of life and beating the Chargers for both league championships.

This being the AFL, the Oilers had their share of colorful characters. And they came in all shapes and sizes.

"Besides Cannon, Charley Tolar had a great year rushing," fullback Dave Smith told *Football Digest*. "He was listed at 5-7 and 195, but I think he was really about 5-5. He ran like a runaway bowling ball.

"One day, we stayed at a hotel where there was a convention of midgets. As a group of us players got off an elevator, there stood Charley waiting to get on, surrounded by several of the delegates to the convention.

"'Look,' Cannon yelled, 'Charley brought his whole family to the game.'"

There was nothing small about the matchup between the Texans and Oilers for the 1962 title. Dallas had gone 11–3 with the most prolific attack in the league and the stingiest defense. Coach Stram's personnel skills, which were exceeded only by his strategic acumen, had put together a roster that even the powerful Oilers could respect: Dawson, Haynes, Robinson, Fred Arbanas, Chris Burford, E. J. Holub, Dave Grayson, and Jerry Mays.

And a kicker named Tommy Brooker.

"The day I drove up in 1962 to Dallas, I had no idea what the team was like the year before," said Brooker, who was a seventeenth-round draft pick that year out of Alabama. "I didn't know the players in the league or any of that. Coach [Bear] Bryant ingrained in me to not really think about the odds of me making the team. If I ever thought about the odds on that, I would not have made it."

Make it he did and not just as a placekicker. Indeed, Brooker's versatility came in handy immediately as well in a historic game two days before Christmas that year.

"I was the top receiver at Alabama my senior year, caught 12 passes and had two TDs," Brooker said. "So I was used some by Coach Stram in the offense, and I caught four passes, three for TDs, as a rookie."

THE OTHER AFL TITLE GAMES

January 1, 1961

Led by George Blanda, the Houston Oilers whipped the Los Angeles Chargers 24–16 in the first AFL championship game. The Oilers' quarterback fired three touchdown passes, including an 88-yarder to Billy Cannon, and kicked an 18-yard field goal.

Blanda, finishing off his twelfth pro season, completed 16 of 31 pass attempts for 301 yards, while Cannon caught three passes for 128 yards.

"It was a real rugged ballgame," said Cannon, voted the game's outstanding player. "Sure, I thought I'd go all the way on that pass."

The Oilers' defense, meanwhile, intercepted two passes by Chargers quarterback Jack Kemp, the league's top passer that season.

"That Blanda is a hell of a guy," said Chargers coach Sid Gillman. "He was the margin of difference today."

And so was the Houston defense.

"It was our best overall game, and our best defensive game all year," Blanda said. "Today we were the best team, but Los Angeles is real good, and they might be able to beat us tomorrow." Ben Agajanian kicked three field goals for the Chargers.

A crowd of 32,183 attended the historic game at Jeppesen Stadium in Houston.

December 24, 1961

The Oilers beat the Chargers, now playing in San Diego, for the second straight year in the AFL title game. Blanda literally did it all for Houston with a touchdown pass, extra-point kick, and 46-yard field goal in the Oilers' 10–3 victory.

The game was a defensive struggle from start to finish as Houston's linebackers kept Chargers quarterback Jack Kemp completely bottled up.

The game was decided when Billy Cannon caught a 35-yard touchdown pass from Blanda early in the third quarter. Cannon, once again voted outstanding player in the championship game, caught five passes for 53 yards and carried the ball 15 times for 48 yards.

The Chargers were upset with the officiating. "It was the worst officiating I've ever seen, at least this season," Gillman said.

Both teams were heavily penalized, particularly the Chargers, who received penalties totaling 106 yards. The Oilers had 68 yards in penalties.

January 5, 1964

Keith Lincoln gained an amazing total of 349 yards as the San Diego Chargers routed the Boston Patriots 51–10. Gillman declared his team "the universal champions," and the beleaguered Patriots couldn't agree more.

"Lincoln is the best back in the league—bar none," said Patriots defensive end Bob Dee. "About five of us hit him and couldn't bring him down."

Hard to believe, but Lincoln's performance came on a day when he wasn't feeling so well.

"I didn't feel real good there early in the game," Lincoln said. "My legs sort of went out after I made those first couple of runs. I just didn't seem to have life in my legs."

To Patriots halfback Ron Burton, the lopsided loss was "embarrassing."

"But we shouldn't feel too bad," he added. "We played a good ball club."

December 26, 1964

The Buffalo Bills shut out the potent San Diego Chargers for an entire half en route to a 20–7 victory in the title game capping the 1964 season.

The Bills' defense was a big part of the story, along with the passing of Jack Kemp, the running of Cookie Gilchrist, and the kicking of Pete Gogolak. The Bills' fans showed their appreciation with 40,242 in attendance at War Memorial Stadium, which had a listed capacity of 37,981.

The contest was played in unusually warm weather for Buffalo, near 50 degrees on a wet field. It didn't have any effect on the Bills' running or passing game.

Although he was injured early in the fourth quarter, Gilchrist managed to gain 122 yards rushing and 22 more on two pass completions. Kemp passed for 188 yards, including a 51-yarder to Glenn Bass to set up a quarterback sneak that clinched the game for the Bills.

Gogolak, the trend-setting soccer-style kicker, booted two field goals and kicked two extra points for Buffalo.

The Bills' defense was at its best when it stopped a Chargers drive inside the five-yard line late in the fourth quarter to clinch the contest.

With 25 seconds to play, fans came roaring out of the stands to level the white wooden goalposts, signifying their team's first championship.

December 26, 1965

The Bills won their second straight AFL title with a 23–0 drubbing of the Chargers in a game that featured a 74-yard punt return by Butch Byrd in the second quarter. It was the first runback for a touchdown in the AFL championship series.

Byrd took a 40-yard punt from John Hadl on his 26 and raced down the sideline to help the Bills build a 14–0 lead at the half—all the points they needed to win the AFL title.

"The punt return really helped us and our pass rushing was great," said Bills coach Lou Saban. "We whipped them in the trenches, meaning up front. We knew we had to."

The Bills' defense was prominent against one of the highest-scoring teams in the AFL. The Chargers were favored by six and a half points but never got inside the Buffalo 25-yard line in the game at San Diego's Balboa Stadium.

"We won by clawing and digging, the way we've won all year," said Kemp, who was released by the Chargers in 1962.

January 1, 1967

The Kansas City Chiefs won the AFL's 1966 championship, routing the Bills 31–7 with the help of a spectacular 72-yard pass interception return by safety Johnny Robinson in the second quarter. Robinson's interception, his eleventh of the season, led to a Chiefs field goal.

"I happened to drop back to the middle of the field, and I read Kemp's eyes," Robinson said of the Bills' quarterback. "I was able to get there."

Defensive back Fred Williamson set up the Chiefs' fourth touchdown when he caused a Buffalo turnover with a violent tackle.

Bills coach Joel Collier summed it up succinctly: "They were much better than we were."

For the first time, the winner of the AFL title game went on to the Super Bowl to face the NFL champion. "We kept playing, and we kept our momentum and didn't have time to think of the Super Bowl," Robinson said. The Chiefs weren't so fortunate in their encounter with the Green Bay Packers, losing 35–10 in the initial interleague championship game.

December 31, 1967

The Oakland Raiders completed the 1967 AFL season with a 40–7 trouncing of the Houston Oilers.

"We got off on the wrong foot," said Oilers coach Wally Lemm. "The Raiders hit harder and executed better."

The Oilers ran into a fierce Oakland defense that shut down their running game. Raiders quarterback Daryle Lamonica, meanwhile, fired two touchdown passes, and former Oiler George Blanda kicked four field goals for Oakland. Blanda's 16 points, including four point-after conversions, were a title game record.

Raiders fullback Hewritt Dixon provided a key play for the Raiders, breaking the game open early in the second quarter with a 69-yard touchdown run around left end.

The Raiders, who didn't fumble and didn't have a pass intercepted, were up 30–0 before the Oilers scored their only touchdown.

December 29, 1968

Joe Namath fired three touchdown passes and Jim Turner kicked two field goals as the New York Jets topped the Raiders 27–23 before an AFL championship game record crowd of 62,627 at windy Shea Stadium.

In a typical battle between these two great rivals, Namath led the Jets back from a 23–20 deficit late in the game with a touchdown pass to Don Maynard.

Namath redeemed himself after having one of his passes intercepted, leading to an Oakland touchdown. The Raiders still had nearly eight minutes to respond behind Daryle Lamonica, but the Jets' defense kept them from crossing the goal line. Overall, the Jets' defense held the Raiders to a net 44 yards rushing.

"Of course I thought we could come back," Namath said in the champagne-drenched locker room.

Ahead of him and his teammates was a place in Super Bowl III and a date with destiny against the Baltimore Colts.

January 4, 1970

The Chiefs picked off three of Daryle Lamonica's passes in the final quarter, including a 63-yard return by Emmitt Thomas, to beat the Raiders 17–7 in the AFL's last game.

Lamonica had an off day in the face of a fierce pass rush, particularly by Aaron Brown. "Aaron and I took more of an inside rush today than ever before," said Brown's linemate, Jerry Mays. "We figured if he wanted to roll out, we'd gamble and let him. We knew inside pressure would bother him more."

During the season, Lamonica had only been dropped for losses a total of 11 times, but the Chiefs brought him down behind the line of scrimmage four times in this AFL title game.

Quarterback Len Dawson led the Kansas City offense, setting up short touchdown runs by Wendell Hayes and Robert Holmes.

Thomas's return, meanwhile, set up Jan Stenerud's 22-yard field goal that provided the killing blow for the Chiefs.

The Chiefs went on to a 23–7 victory over the Minnesota Vikings in Super Bowl IV to tie the interleague series at two games apiece. It was the final meeting between the AFL and the NFL before the leagues merged under one umbrella and started to play a common schedule.

One of those was against Denver, for 92 yards, the longest in Chiefs history until Mark Boerigter beat it in 2002 with a 99-yarder. For Brooker, that was his most memorable play—until December 23, 1962, when the Texans and Oilers made their own kind of history.

Recalling the 92-yard touchdown play, Brooker said, "We were playing on a baseball field, Bears Stadium in Denver, and the weather was awful, a real mess. I would take a step and slide because we were playing in the mud and the rain and the snow. I would take a step, then slide, another step and slide, and got all the way to the end zone that way."

While his three touchdowns in four receptions were remarkable that season, Brooker truly was most effective as a kicker, one of the many weapons Stram could call on.

Houston also was 11–3, but one of those defeats was an embarrassing rout—at home—against the Texans. Dawson threw for three touchdowns in a 31–7 romp the Oilers found so humiliating that they were thoroughly motivated to make up for it. They didn't lose another game during the season.

Facing the Texans for the championship was a juicy proposition for the Oilers, who with a victory could claim three successive titles, something only one NFL team—the Green Bay Packers—had managed since that league was established in 1922. And they could do it against their biggest rival, no small feat in the state where everything is considered bigger by the Lone Star inhabitants.

"We had two championships already, so we knew we were the best the league had," Hennigan said.

Not that the Oilers were getting cocky. Dave Smith called the Texans "a tough crew."

"They had guys like Len Dawson, Chris Burford, Jack Spikes, and Jerry Mays. That E. J. Holub was healthy then, and what a linebacker he was!

"They also had a real tough back in Abner Haynes. One day I went down under a punt, and that Haynes turned me around so many times I didn't know which way I was going."

Both teams knew they were headed for Jeppesen Stadium for the title game.

Jeppesen was not exactly a crown jewel in Houston. Oilers owner Bud Adams wanted to play at Rice Stadium, but the university would not allow a pro team to use the on-campus facility; that would change in 1965.

So Jeppesen, which eventually became Robertson Stadium, home of the University of Houston Cougars, was the Oilers' early home.

And not a very pleasant place to play.

Al Jamison, a cocaptain of the 1962 Oilers, recalled Jeppesen Stadium as the second-rate pro football facility it was.

"I remember playing there in three inches of mud," said Jamison. "The TV people came in and dyed the turf green. Everything we had was covered in green mud."

Weather and playing conditions would become almost a decisive factor during the championship game. First, though, Dallas went up 17–0 at halftime. Dawson, an NFL castoff, calmly led the Texans to that impressive lead. His counterpart, the highly accomplished Blanda, an AFL all-star after a solid career in the NFL, threw two costly interceptions.

"Didn't play worth a darn," Blanda said of the first half.

The next two, uh, three quarters, would be dramatically different— on the field and off.

"We went in at halftime 17–0 against a team that had won the first two league championships," Brooker recalled. "We were feeling good.

"Then, the odd thing that happened is the weather and how it turned at halftime. There were tornado warnings out, the wind was unbelievable. It was awful, the field was so sloppy. It was a wonder nobody got blown away and that we were able to finish the game."

They call them "Blue Northers," and Dawson admitted that he "never knew what they were until that day." He would never forget.

"When a Blue Norther comes through Texas, boy, it is cold and windy," Chiefs executive Jack Steadman explained. "Nasty.

"So the second half of the game was played under terrible weather conditions."

Tuesdays and Thursdays, I used to go down to the Bills' office and sweep up. That's the joke that [teammate] Paul Maguire would use when he would introduce me [at speaking engagements].

The 1965 championship game against the San Diego Chargers stands out.

During the season, when we played the Chargers in Buffalo, they kicked our butts. We just couldn't get out of our own way on offense. And so when we went out to California for the championship game, everybody thought it was just going to be a pushover for the Chargers, that all they would have to do is show up and throw their helmets on the field. But we had a special game plan; the defense knew they had to have their heads in the game.

And I think what set the tone is a great play that Booker Edgerson made on Lance Alworth. He was the receiver they called Bambi because they said he ran like a deer and couldn't be caught from behind.

Well, Alworth ran a quick post pattern on Booker, our cornerback. Alworth got one or two steps on Booker, caught the pass, and looked like he was off to the races for a touchdown. But Booker just ran him down and caught him from behind on about the 10-yard line. I think Alworth was so shocked he was caught from behind that he fumbled the football into the end zone and we recovered. That killed them. They took their best shot, and we turned it against them [and won the game 23–0].

right to me; he had no idea I was there. It surprised me, but I wasn't about to drop it."

Hull scooted 23 yards to midfield, stopping the Oilers' drive and sending the teams into a second overtime still tied at 17.

Spikes, who'd lost much of his playing time during the season to McClinton, gained 29 yards on successive plays, and it was time to turn to Brooker.

Was there any concern that the rookie couldn't handle the pressure, even if the field goal would be only 25 yards?

"Tommy never missed a PAT in his whole career," Dawson said, "and this was kind of like an extra point."

Piece of cake, Brooker thought. And pretty much said.

"We called a time-out to plan to kick the field goal," he remembered. "Lenny Dawson was the holder and E.J. the snapper, and Curtis McClinton was the rookie fullback blocking. We were standing in the huddle, and Lenny was on his knees cleaning out my cleats on the ground in preparation for me to kick. You could hear a pin drop in that huddle. Nobody was saying if I would make it or not make it.

"So I said, 'It's over.'

"Some writers later said I was a brash rookie, and I was. But I was confident because I needed to be confident. Coach Bryant taught us that confidence."

Perfect snap, impeccable blocking, and a dead-on kick at 2 minutes, 54 seconds, into the second overtime.

Wow! Dallas 20, Houston 17.

The Texans were AFL champs in the longest pro football game up to that time.

One wag called the five-plus period drama the AFL's version of *The Longest Day*, a popular film of the time about the D-Day invasion during World War II. Brooker called it something else: truly the greatest game ever played.

"I think my championship game was more exciting than the Colts–Giants game," he said. "I saw that on TV recently, and it didn't compare to ours."

Brooker is constantly being reminded of that, especially at team get-together events.

"One time, I was at a reunion and had my son with me, and the first one we saw was Abner Haynes. Abner made a comment about that game and the coin toss: 'I screwed it up.'

"And I said, 'Yeah, and I had to clear it up for [you] by kicking the field goal.'"

7

AFL Rivalries

The Oakland game was a tougher physical battle than the Super Bowl. The emotion of it was unreal.

—Former New York Jets coach Walt Michaels

It was the 1960s when "Broadway Joe" met the "Mad Bomber."

Joe Namath versus Daryle Lamonica. The New York Jets versus the Oakland Raiders, a rivalry with no holds barred.

"I always enjoyed playing against Joe because we both liked to put the ball in the air and make the game exciting," said Lamonica, known as the Mad Bomber for obvious reasons.

The Jets and Raiders played each other twice a year in the 1960s—a game on each coast. And Lamonica and Namath, the flamboyant "Broadway Joe," never met a pass they didn't like.

The rivalry reached fever pitch when the Raiders broke Namath's jaw in a 1967 game. Raiders coach Al Davis and Jets coach Weeb Ewbank kept the fires burning with their own personal rivalry—no love lost between the two.

Davis's feelings were obvious. For many years, he had an enlarged photo hung at Raiders headquarters showing Namath sprawled on the field, his helmet flying, after a vicious Raiders hit.

"The Raiders were always a cheap-shot bunch taking shots at Joe," remembered the Jets' Larry Grantham. "On defense, we would react pretty unfavorably to it and get one of theirs if they got one of ours. Lamonica was there with that long arm action, and I'm sure he took a few retaliation hits.

"One of their defensive ends, Ben Davidson, broke Joe's jaw on a play well after it was over. So we got up in arms and it was ironic and sweet to beat them [27–23 in 1968] and go to the Super Bowl."

Jon Schmitt was part of an offensive line that tried to keep Namath out of harm's way. They played with a sense of mission that reached beyond their job description.

"The quickest way to beat our team was to hurt Joe," Schmitt says. "We had a love for him that we had for no one else. And Ben Davidson was a cheap-shot artist. We had a lot of reasons to hate those guys. They're probably the only team we ever felt that way about. At the time, if I could have run Ben Davidson over with a car and laughed, I would have."

The Jets weren't the Raiders' only big rival. Another red-hot rivalry existed with the Kansas City Chiefs in their own Western Division. These rivalries became hot tempered in the mid- to late 1960s, when all three teams developed into powerhouses.

The Chiefs were also involved in other strong rivalries earlier in the decade when they were first known as the Dallas Texans.

"San Diego and Houston were the main ones early on," remembered Len Dawson, the Chiefs' Hall of Fame quarterback. "Oakland was not very good until Al Davis got there, then he changed things around."

A three-sided rivalry developed between the Oilers, Chargers, and Texans at the beginning of the decade. The Oilers won the AFL's first championship when they beat the Chargers, then located in Los Angeles. They repeated the following season after the Chargers had moved to San Diego. The Texans knocked off the Oilers in the third AFL season in one of the most memorable games in the league's history: a 20–17 double-overtime thriller, at the time the longest game in pro football.

"The Chargers were in our division and the best team," Dawson remembered of the AFL's early years. "With Houston, we would have that rivalry because of both teams being in Texas, and a lot of Texans were on both teams."

The Raiders–Jets rivalry was especially compelling when Lamonica and Namath hooked up in one of their high-flying aerial shows.

"Those were always the most physical games, like both lines trying to beat up the guy on the other side, and the Raiders always were trying to get after me the way we were trying to get after Daryle Lamonica," Namath said. "You came out of a Raiders game knowing you'd played a tough, physical football team that wasn't afraid to cross the line.

"The idea that guys could always get hurt was always there but even more so when you played the Raiders. And it always wound up being a real good football game, too. Both teams really got up for each other because we played twice a year, so it was a rivalry even with one team on each coast."

Lamonica and Namath always seemed to be playing against each other when something was on the line.

Lamonica, a product of Notre Dame, was a backup to Jack Kemp at Buffalo for a couple of years before his trade to Oakland in 1967.

"I was very excited about the trade, but at the same time, hurt from the standpoint that the Bills had given up on me," Lamonica said. "It's funny, but I had talked to Ralph Wilson Jr., the owner of the Bills, just the night before. And he had said the team was looking forward to me coming back and helping win another championship. So I was excited about that, but in eight hours, I was traded. So it was sort of a shock."

No more of a shock than the Bills received when Lamonica turned into one of the league's star quarterbacks. It happened almost overnight—that same season, in fact, when he was voted the AFL's most valuable player. Two years later, he won that award again.

But even with all the accolades, Lamonica wasn't in Namath's class financially. No one was.

Coming out of Alabama as one of the most hyped players in AFL history, Namath signed an over-the-top contract with the Jets.

The deal, for $400,000, sent shock waves throughout pro football.

"I believe it is the largest amount ever given to an athlete for professional services," Jets president Sonny Werblin told the press.

Stealing Namath away from the NFL was a tremendous victory for the AFL and generally regarded as one of the turning points that led to the merger of the two leagues.

BOOKER EDGERSON

Booker Edgerson was a Buffalo Bills defensive back from 1962 to 1969 and played on AFL championship teams in 1964 and 1965. He closed out his career with two years in Denver. During the off-season, Edgerson taught school. Following retirement, education played a big part in his life. Following short careers with his own travel agency and as a marketing representative with IBM, Edgerson joined Erie Community College, where he held the position of director of equity and diversity for 24 years.

My starting position was at cornerback, and I was also the safety valve on the kickoff teams and the punt team. So I was basically the safety valve to make sure that nobody got beyond and scored touchdowns on us.

You had to play more than one position—that was the nature of the game back then. Now these guys are specialists. You've got a long snapper, that's all he does is snap the ball . . . on punts, extra points, and field goals. You've got guys on special teams. That's all they do is special teams.

The game's a lot different with the training and the coaching aspect. We had four coaches when I came in. Now they've got 24 coaches. I don't know what they do with all those coaches. Does it take that many coaches to lose?

The players today are stronger because of the weight programs. In a lot of cases, they're better because they're able to stay in shape year-round. We had to get a job in the off-season in order to support ourselves because we weren't making any money. You went to camp to get in shape. These guys today go to camp already in shape because they work out year-round.

They didn't start using weights in Buffalo until 1968, and that was because one of the draft choices came here and said, "Where's the weights?" In colleges, they had the weight programs and everything. And he was a high draft choice, so they started putting the weight program together. Prior to that, we didn't have a weight program . . . go out there and get some cement blocks and move them around.

We had an outstanding defense, bar none. So when the offense couldn't move the ball, it didn't make any difference because the other team's offense wasn't going to move the ball, either, because we wouldn't allow it to happen.

We also had a very mature offense that was not selfish, either. Our quarterback, Jack Kemp, was a great thinker and a hell of a passer. He was a good leader, he talked to the ballplayers, he kept things going. And it all came together under Lou Saban.

What stands out are the '64, '65 championships. You just can't beat those two championship games or those championship years.

San Diego was a premier team. Big, strong. Everyone thought California teams were better. They called Cleveland the "armpit of the East," and Buffalo was in second place. Nobody gave us any respect, but what it all came down to was that we had no prima donnas on the team. We had a lot of cohesiveness. The players stuck together. It wasn't basically individual statistics. It was all about winning.

"We were just destroying ourselves with the open checkbook, and we needed to have some controls over our player costs," Cleveland Browns owner Art Modell said of the escalating salaries in the signing war between the two leagues.

In terms of publicity, Namath's signing was worth every penny to the AFL. Especially his personal battles against Lamonica and the Raiders.

Their most memorable battle: the *Heidi* game of 1968.

"That game probably gave me more satisfaction, knowing that we never did quit," Lamonica said. "From a quarterback's standpoint, it was a wonderful game."

Not so wonderful from the Jets' standpoint. They led 32–29 with 65 seconds left.

At that point, the NBC network went to a commercial break. TV viewers settled back to watch the end of this exciting game.

Not so fast.

When the commercial ended, viewers were shocked to find that NBC had terminated the game's broadcast. In its place, the network started airing a TV version of the famous children's story of the little Swiss miss.

This was no fairy tale. It left millions of football fans across the nation puzzled and angry. Angrier still when they later found out they had missed one of the greatest finishes in AFL history.

The Raiders scored two touchdowns in nine seconds and won the game 43–32.

"I know it blew a lot of circuits in New York," Lamonica said. "Of course we didn't know anything about it at the time. We were just trying to win a football game."

A TV executive had ordered the switch to fulfill a contractual arrangement to start showing *Heidi* at precisely 7:00 p.m. Eastern Standard Time. Phones from outraged football fans rang off the hook. This included the president of NBC at the time, Julian Goodman, but it was too late to reestablish a video link.

"I missed the end of the game as much as anyone else," Goodman said.

And what an ending!

Lamonica unleashed a 43-yard touchdown pass to Charlie Smith, and George Blanda kicked the extra point for a 36–32 Raiders lead.

There were 42 seconds left, enough time for the strong-armed Namath to move the Jets for a touchdown.

But Earl Christy fumbled the Raiders' low kickoff, and special teams player Preston Ridlehuber recovered the fumble and took the ball into the end zone for an Oakland touchdown.

"We worked on this particular pass play with Smith all week," Lamonica recalled of his late touchdown pass, his fourth of the game, "and we knew if we caught the right defense, it would work."

While Lamonica was throwing touchdown passes, football fans were throwing tantrums when the game was taken off the air and supplanted by *Heidi*.

"It was a forgivable error made by human beings who were concerned about the children expecting to see *Heidi* at 7 p.m.," Goodman said.

The game was a confidence builder for the Raiders.

"It just proved to me and my teammates that if we'd hang in there, we could make things happen," Lamonica said. "We fought adversity, had a touchdown pass called back, and still never gave up. And that year, we went on to win our division."

The *Heidi* game made a lasting impact on professional football, in effect changing the way the sport was covered on television. Games would now be shown in their entirety—never again would a network cut away from a contest just to broadcast a previously scheduled show on time. The NFL, now merged with the AFL, actually had such language written into its TV contract.

Namath turned the tables on Lamonica the next time they met on December 29, 1968, knocking off the Raiders 27–23 in the AFL championship game.

Then it was on to a stunning upset of the Baltimore Colts in Super Bowl III, one of the most important games in pro football history.

At first, the Raiders–Chiefs rivalry wasn't much of a rivalry at all.

"[Their team] was so bad that [Chiefs owner] Lamar Hunt traded Cotton Davidson [to the Raiders] to help them try to survive," Dawson said. "We'd heard that Lamar loaned the Raiders money to keep going, too."

The Chiefs' rivalry with the Raiders didn't really begin until Davis got to Oakland in 1963 and started turning around the team.

"We won the division in '66, and at that time we already had a pretty big rivalry between us and the Raiders and put San Diego in the mix," Dawson said. "When both teams got pretty strong, both were pretty physical and had outstanding defenses, and we could really run the ball and pound it at people."

The Raiders–Chiefs rivalry truly developed into a great one when both teams were peaking in the late 1960s. In 1969, the Raiders beat the Chiefs twice during the season, including a 27–24 thriller that San Francisco sportswriter Glenn Dickey called "the best football game I ever saw."

It was a battle for first place in the AFL's Western Division between two of the best teams in football. The Raiders fell behind 14–3, tied the game 17–17 at the half, and charged ahead 27–17 after three quarters.

Oakland's defense played a big role in this meeting of AFL powerhouses, turning two interceptions of Len Dawson passes into touchdowns. The Chiefs rallied to make it 27–24 and had an opportunity to tie or win the game at the end, but rookie Ed Podolak fumbled away a punt with 1:45 left. The Raiders held on for a three-point victory.

"The Kansas City Chiefs turned the tomahawk upon themselves today and gave away a game and first place in the American Football

League's Western Division to the Oakland Raiders," wrote William Wallace in the *New York Times*.

In the final regular-season game of 1969, the Chiefs lost a bitter 10–6 decision to the Raiders. Dawson's health problems played a big part in the game.

"I must have thrown only six or eight passes," Dawson said. "My knee had been a problem that year, and Hank wanted me as the quarterback in the playoffs. Some of our guys were perturbed we kept the wraps on it.

"Hank would always say, 'We will attack them on the ground.' And I was saying, 'Let's try to bombard them through the air.'"

Their playoff meeting was another story. The Raiders went into the game with injuries to key players. Warren Wells, one of the Raiders' top receivers and their main deep threat, was injured, and Lamonica played with a bruised thumb.

"It happened on the follow-through of a pass," Dickey remembered. "But [John] Madden was a rookie coach, and he didn't have that much confidence in [backup George] Blanda after Lamonica was hurt. So he just let Lamonica stay in there, bruised thumb and all, and Lamonica couldn't really throw the ball that effectively."

The result: a 17–7 victory for the Chiefs over the Raiders and a spot in the fourth pro football championship game between the NFL and AFL, which they eventually won.

"When you played the Raiders, you just tried to avoid getting hurt," Dawson said. "There were guys on our team who truly did not like them. I never had the personal feeling, but I didn't ever turn my back on them after a play. Their philosophy was to take a cheap shot at the quarterback and see if you can knock him out of the game. Even if you get a 15-yard penalty.

"The rules then were different, and you could block the quarterback on an interception. I knew if I threw an interception, two or three of those defensive linemen were coming after me, no matter where I went and where the guy who intercepted was headed."

Dawson said that Davis, the Raiders' longtime boss, "brings out the worst in everybody."

"I remember our guys getting ready for a game with them and [coach] Hank [Stram] wanting to beat them badly," Dawson added. "We'd think that it was just another game, and he'd say, 'No, this is Raider Week, these are the Raiders, it is different.' I thought, 'Should we bring our brass knuckles?'"

8

Opening Doors

The AFL didn't exactly hang out a banner, but it could have: "Black football players—welcome to the AFL!"

Lionel Taylor had played a partial season for the NFL's Chicago Bears in 1959 when he was cut by George Halas.

"When I was released, Halas said he had players from bigger schools he had to keep, so I left," Taylor recalled. "He was telling me I was a good football player, but I was the one getting on a Trailways bus back home."

No matter. Taylor joined the Denver Broncos of the newly established AFL and went on to a spectacular career. He was the first AFL receiver to catch 100 passes in one season, led the league in receptions for the first six years of its existence, and retired as the AFL's all-time leading receiver with 567 catches.

Without the AFL, Taylor probably would have a different story to tell.

As a black football player, the doors were open wider for him in the AFL than the NFL, according to Taylor.

"When I was with Chicago, there were four black players with the Bears. But most teams in the AFL had quite a few black players, a lot more than the NFL teams."

The NFL did most of its recruiting in the bigger schools from the major college conferences, which were virtually all white.

The AFL did the same. But the new league also aggressively recruited the talent in historically smaller black colleges, while the NFL was nowhere near as active in this area.

"It opened the doors for the black athlete, say what you want to say," said Taylor, who played at New Mexico Highlands. "It was a gigantic step.

"The NFL didn't have to go to those smaller schools. The AFL went after those players because they wanted to and they needed to."

Lamar Hunt, just as he was a trailblazer in starting the AFL, also made it a point to hire a scout who concentrated strictly on the black colleges, Lloyd Wells.

"Lamar had gone to any game that was in the Cotton Bowl, and Grambling would play in the Cotton Bowl every year with other black colleges," said Jack Steadman, Hunt's longtime top business executive. "Lamar felt there were some great, great players that were overlooked because they were black."

For example, Abner Haynes from North Texas State. Another, Buck Buchanan from Grambling State University. Still another, Willie Lanier from Morgan State.

"Imagine if there had been no AFL and no Kansas City Chiefs," Lanier told *Sports Illustrated*. "Maybe I have to wait five years for my chance [to play in the NFL], for the chance to play middle linebacker. And five years in football is an eternity."

Lanier didn't have to wait long to be inducted into the Pro Football Hall of Fame. He was honored in 1986 for a career as one of the most devastating and intelligent players of his generation.

Lanier, nicknamed "Contact" for the force of his tackles, played the middle linebacker position for the Chiefs for 11 seasons. Every year from 1968 through 1975, the 6-foot-1, 245-pound Lanier was either all-pro, all-AFL, or all-AFC.

The Chiefs were among the most active in recruiting black athletes. By 1966, Kansas City's starting lineup featured eight blacks among the 22 players. That team won the AFL championship.

In a comparison between the teams in the 1970 Super Bowl, the official game program showed Kansas City with 19 black players and Minnesota with 10.

"We really focused on scouting the black colleges," Steadman said. "We found some real talent out of those colleges. I think that started it more than anything. It was just looking for talent. It wasn't a point of, 'Well, we're going to bring in black players,' it was a point of finding players who could compete and play well."

Lanier knew he had come to the right place in Kansas City when he was given a fair shot by coach Hank Stram at middle linebacker, which at that point was almost exclusively white.

"Hank said, 'If you are the best, you will be our middle linebacker,'" recalled quarterback Len Dawson. "Willie and the black players appreciated that thinking."

In open competition against Notre Dame's Jim Lynch, Lanier won the job and became the first black middle linebacker in pro football. Lynch became a starter at outside linebacker.

There were other firsts for black players in pro football, thanks to the AFL. Gene Mingo of the Denver Broncos, for instance, was pro football's first black placekicker. Grambling's Buck Buchanan was the first black leaguewide number one draft choice in the pros.

By comparison, the NFL's New York Giants waited until the nineteenth round to select Buchanan, the 265th overall pick in its draft.

"There was a rumor that there was an unwritten law in the NFL: no more than five black players [per team]," said Chargers lineman Ron Mix, who is white. "I don't know if it was true or not, but there weren't that many black players in the NFL on each team."

Clearly, the NFL was not making any extra effort to bring in black players. In the AFL, they were just color blind.

"They couldn't afford not to be color blind," Mix said. "They needed to bring in the best talent. I wasn't part of any decision-making process, but I could only look at what the end result was: there were far more black players per team in the AFL than there was in the NFL."

Washington Redskins owner George Preston Marshall may have been part of the reason. One of the NFL's more influential figures, he refused to sign a black player until he was pressured by the Kennedy administration in 1962.

The AFL, on the other hand, welcomed all of the black players from smaller schools with open arms.

"They saw they had an opportunity to play," said Larry Garron. "They weren't going to be used just as blocking dummies to let the other guys get ready for their season."

Garron was one of those players from a small school given a solid chance in the AFL. And he proved worthy. As a fullback with the

ALL-STAR BOYCOTT

The bus was about to leave for the first practice of the 1964 AFL All-Star Game.

Sid Gillman, coach of the West team, started calling roll.

"Abner Haynes."

No response.

"Willie Lanier."

No response.

"Earl Faison . . . Ernie Ladd . . . Buck Buchanan."

Again, no response.

None of the black players are here," one player said.

"Yeah, they're all meeting," said somebody else.

"They're talking about boycotting the game."

"Why?" Gillman asked.

The answer: in their abbreviated time in New Orleans, the black players had faced the ugly specter of racism.

"New Orleans was a segregated city at the time," said Ron Mix, who represented the San Diego Chargers in the West lineup. "The black players were having a hard time getting cabs from the airport. Cab drivers wouldn't pick them up. Then when they went out to try and get food, they were turned away from all the restaurants."

As the Chargers' Dick Westmoreland emphasized, "People shouted insults, and doors were shut in our faces."

Mix asked Gillman if he could be excused from practice to go over and talk to the black players.

"I got off the bus and went to the place where they were meeting."

Mix was sympathetic to the black cause but thought it would be best for them to play the game in New Orleans and call national attention to what was going on.

The blacks were adamant in their feelings, in particular, Buffalo's Cookie Gilchrist.

"No, it's gone too far," he said. "We're not going to play in this town. Time to take a stand."

"Okay," Mix said. "If that's the way you feel about it, count me in. I'll join you."

Thus began the first and only boycott of an American city due to a sports event. The black players, perhaps emboldened by the Civil Rights Act of 1964, made their statement in a big way.

It reflected a time of social change in America. The 1960s featured such events as the 1963 March on Washington, forced integration of schools, a number of sit-ins, riots, and "Freedom Rides."

There were 21 protesting players in all involved in this sports version of the Freedom Ride.

The AFL decided to reverse its field, pull out of New Orleans, and replant the game in nearby Houston.

"Everything went smoothly," said Buffalo Bills safety George Saimes. "We got on planes, flew to Houston, they had hotels for us, no problem, and the game was played."

The negative publicity didn't seem to hurt New Orleans's hopes of landing an NFL franchise. The city had an NFL team just a few years later, in 1967.

Mix felt that the boycott eventually helped to desegregate the city.

"They knew now they weren't [going] to get an NFL franchise unless they desegregated the city," Mix said. "That's what they did. It was desegregated ahead of schedule."

The 1964 All-Star Game, actually played on January 16, 1965, had become the secondary story.

For the record:

A crowd of 15,448 at Jeppesen Stadium in Houston watched John Hadl toss three touchdown passes and Keith Lincoln score twice as the West beat the East 38–14.

Boston Patriots in the early 1960s, he was a four-time AFL all-star and on the Patriots' AFL Decade Team.

Actually, Garron was more than just a fullback.

"I played eight different positions: all the positions in the defensive backfield, and on offense, I was a split end, a tight end, a fullback, and a halfback," Garron said.

Before turning to football, Garron had designs on becoming a basketball player. He originally had a basketball scholarship to Kansas.

"I went down and met the athletic director. He said, 'Okay, did you bring Garron?' All the time they thought I was bigger. I was

5-foot-10, I was able to jump over the basket, and they thought I was big. I was a guard and a forward.

"The athletic director said, 'Let me introduce you to your competition.' And this tall guy came through the door—Wilt Chamberlain, that's who I competed against. We laughed, but a lot of people don't know, I qualified for the Olympics in track. In the Drake Relays, Wilt and I competed against each other in the high jump and the quarter-mile relays."

Garron became a brilliant football player in the pros, but he wasn't quite sure he would even be able to make a college football team at first.

"Our quarterback in high school had gone on to Western Illinois," Garron remembered. "He thought I'd have the opportunity to make the team, and he'd have a chance to throw to me. And so I went down on a biology scholarship, never did have an athletic scholarship, and they ran out of money after a year. I had to work for the remaining three years."

While in college, Garron had made an important connection with coach Lou Saban. They would connect again, in the pros.

Garron had three NFL teams interested in him but wound up with the AFL's Patriots because of Saban.

"As soon as he heard he was going to be head coach with Boston in '58, he signed me to come to Boston," Garron recalled. "I was so fortunate to have three teams in the National Football League ask for me. But I felt I had a better opportunity going with my coach who was also a National Football League coach, who was familiar enough with both systems."

Garron was a good fit with the Patriots' style, which also happened to be the general style of the AFL.

"One of the big things we did was open it up with passes," Garron said. "And that was a big thing because if you look at the National Football League, it was basically on the ground, running the ball. In the NFL, it was one or two running plays, and then it was kick, kick, kick."

Not so in the AFL.

"With us, it was a little deceptive running and passing. It paid off quite well. I played a little quarterback when I was in high school and college, and the running halfback pass play was a big thing when we played."

Quarterback Babe Parilli expertly steered the offense.

"Our opponents had to watch a lot of people," Garron said.

That included Garron, who was not only a force as a running back but also a receiver. In the Patriots' media guide of 1968, Parilli called Garron "one of the best backs at catching passes I have ever played with."

Saban started to improve the team with his savvy coaching.

"He saw that we had speed, and with speed you can throw passes," Garron said. "That put us on the map."

Garron's greatest season: 1963.

"I was healthy again. Many people didn't realize it, but the first year we were out in California, I collapsed. I had 103-degree fever. I had tonsillitis.

"Lou released me and sent me back. I came back the next year. I was living in Boston and I worked out at the Huntington YMCA. A couple of weight lifters there taught me how to lift weights. With the training, I got back in shape. I was 167, 168 pounds when I left California. When I went back to the team, I was 215. And then it went on from there. It was great."

Garron led the Patriots with 750 yards rushing and gained 418 yards receiving, returned kicks for 693 yards for a 24.8 average, and also returned a punt 23 yards.

Garron wasn't the only African American player who made an impact with the Patriots. Remembers Jon Morris, an all-pro center for the Pats, "At Holy Cross, we didn't have any black players. And so when I went to the Patriots, I'd say that 30 percent of the team was black. I started to look at them and said, 'Man, these guys can play!' And not only that, but they were pretty good guys. You just don't know because you've never been associated with them.

"There were great players at places like Grambling and Texas A&I and other colleges because the big-time football schools in the South wouldn't take the black guy."

Morris recalled the contributions of Garron, Houston Antwine, Jim Hunt, and Don Webb, among others.

"These guys were all great players, and nobody knew it. The rest of them came from small schools, and nobody knew who they were. And so the AFL gave them a chance to show what they could do. And they really took advantage of it, no question about it."

Lance Alworth, who grew up in the South picking cotton in the summer alongside blacks in Mississippi and Louisiana, also recognized the black talent at that time.

ELBERT DUBENION

Elbert Dubenion was a wide receiver for the Buffalo Bills from 1960 to 1968. He was an AFL all-star in 1964 and was on the receiving end of a 93-yard touchdown play, the longest in AFL playoff history. Dubenion had his breakout season in 1964 when he scored 10 touchdowns. That year, Dubenion had 42 receptions for 1,139 yards. Nicknamed "Dubey" and "Golden Wheels," Dubenion went on to become an NFL scout for the Bills, Miami Dolphins, and Atlanta Falcons.

Playing for Bluffton College, I was a running back. It took me a while to adjust to catching the ball as a wide receiver in the pros, missing as many as I caught the first couple of years. I was the first player from Bluffton to play pro ball. The *only* player.

I dropped so many balls in my first year, I could hardly play I was so nervous. I was so scared. I hoped they didn't throw the ball to me. Buster Ramsey was my coach—he was the line coach of the Detroit Lions. He cursed a lot. See, Bluffton was a Christian college—they didn't do that at Bluffton.

When I went to the All-Star Game in Chicago to play the Baltimore Colts, I had never seen so many big guys in all my life. I was about the third biggest guy on my team at Bluffton, at 180 pounds. The Colts had Gino Marchetti and all those guys.

We had a play where I was supposed to block Marchetti. Otto Graham was the head coach, and John Wooten was the pulling guard. Coach Graham asked Wooten, "On this play, what do you do when Dubey blocks Marchetti?"

"Well, coach, while Marchetti's killing him, we'll just run to the other side."

With the Bills, I did everything. I caught passes, returned kickoffs, and all for just $7,000 a year.

People ask me about the 93-yard touchdown catch. That was in a playoff game against the Boston Patriots. Daryle Lamonica threw that pass. We called it a "Street Pattern." Anytime a guy tried to cover me one on one, most of the time a quarterback would signal me that we would use that play. It just so happened, it was one-on-one coverage, and Daryle gave me the sign, and I got lucky enough to catch it. It was straight down the right side. Daryle threw it, and I was thrilled that I held on to the ball. It made up for my fumble of the opening kickoff.

The highlight for me was the 1964 season. I averaged 27 yards a catch. For that, I think I got a thousand-dollar raise. It took me nearly five, six years to get double digits. Back then, I started out at $7,000, $7,500, $8,000. I asked a guy, "When do we ever get to double digits?" He said I was from a small school, so I wasn't going to make much more. Don't know if he was BS'n me or not. My backup was making more than I was making. I know one guy, Ray Abruzzese from Alabama, one day he said, "Dub, they took $43 in New York State taxes out of my check." I knew they only took $23 out of mine.

I didn't make a lot of money. There were guys behind me making twice the salary I was making. But I would have probably played for nothing.

I loved the Buffalo fans. They treated me great. They could have easily run me out of town because I dropped so many passes. They called me Golden Wheels, not Golden Hands. But they stuck with me, and I finally got around to catching more passes.

"The guys [at the historically black schools] were just great athletes, just like now you look at all the universities in Florida with all the great athletes. It was the same way back then [for the black schools]; you just had to give the guys the opportunity to be recognized. They wouldn't have gotten a chance to play if the AFL was not around."

The NFL, of course, wasn't completely oblivious to the great black football talent in America.

Paul Brown's dominant early Cleveland teams in the All-America Football Conference and then the NFL featured such black stars as Jim Brown and Marion Motley.

Paul Brown had a link to the historically black schools. One strong relationship developed between the Browns' legendary coach and Eddie Robinson, the Grambling coach.

"Eddie Robinson was a friend of my dad, and he would come to practices with our teams," said Mike Brown, Paul Brown's son and owner of the Cincinnati Bengals. "So we were definitely aware of these players.

"In those days, the southern black kids couldn't go to an SEC [Southeastern Conference] team, so they went to the predominantly black schools, but they were totally black schools in those days."

Among other NFL teams, the Dallas Cowboys were fairly active in scouting the black schools for football talent.

"We hired Dick Mansberger, who went to all these black schools, and we got a bunch of guys from Morgan State, Elizabeth City Teachers College, Johnson C. Smith, those kind of schools," said longtime Dallas Cowboys chief talent scout Gil Brandt. "And these were very good players. It was kind of an unmined gold mine."

Judging by statistics from a variety of sources, the AFL apparently dug deeper in these mines.

"The opening up of the lines to those schools was a big move for the black players," Taylor said. "That was a great contribution to the sport and to the black athletes. I didn't talk much about it back then, but I was proud of it and knew it was there, that the doors were open much more in the AFL than they were in the NFL."

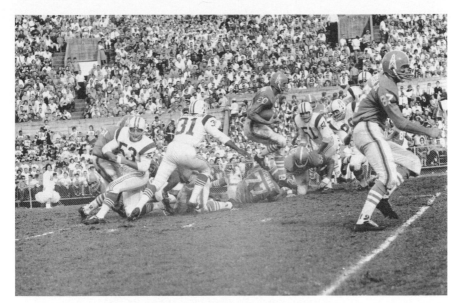

Billy Cannon (20), Houston Oilers halfback, jumps through a hole in the line after taking a handoff from quarterback George Blanda in first quarter action against the Boston Patriots in an American Football League game, November 12, 1961. Cannon picked up 11 yards before he was hit by Boston's Bob Dee (89) and Frank Robotti (51) with Clyde Washington (31) coming up for the tie-down. AP Photo

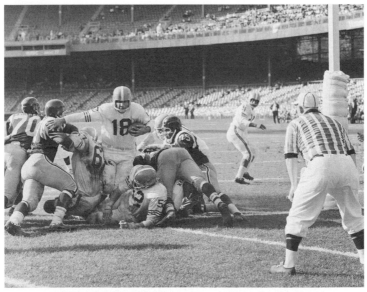

Denver Broncos quarterback Frank Tripucka (18) drives through the New York Titan line standing up to score on a one-yard plunge in the fourth quarter of an American Football League game, September 30, 1962, in New York. Denver linemen Bob McCullough (67) and center Jim Carton (52) are guarding. Identifiable Titans are tackle Gene Cockrell (70), extreme left, and tackle Proverb Jacobs (75), far right. Denver won 32–10. AP Photo/Jerry Mosey

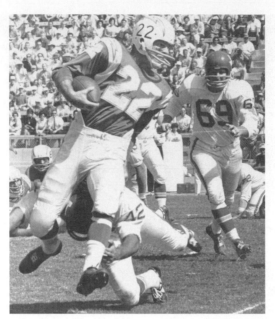

San Diego Chargers fullback Keith Lincoln (22) evades Dallas Texan Johnny Robinson (42) during AFL action at San Diego, October 7, 1962. In pursuit is Texan Sherrill Headrick (69). Lincoln gained 85 yards in 19 carries as the Chargers won 32–28, snapping Dallas' three-game winning streak. AP Photo

Dallas Texan end Tommy Brooker waves as he rides on the shoulders of teammates following the American Football League championship game between the Texans and the Houston Oilers at Houston, Sunday, December 23, 1962. Brooker kicked a 25-yard field goal to win the game 20–17. At right is back Bobby Hunt (20); the lad on the left is not identified. AP Photo

Dallas Texan coach Hank Stram gets a champagne shower in the dressing room after his Texans won the AFL championship by defeating the Houston Oilers 20–17, Sunday, December 24, 1963, in Houston. AP Photo

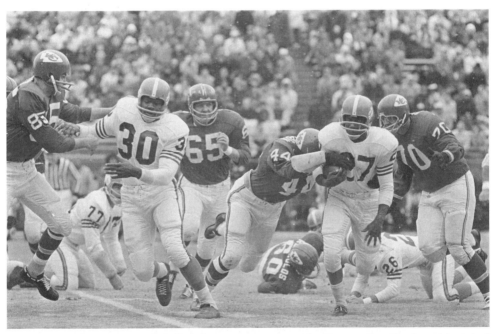

Denver Broncos' Charley Mitchell (27) in action against the Kansas City Chiefs at Municipal Stadium in Kansas City, Missouri, December 8, 1963. Rich Clarkson/Rich Clarkson Associates via AP Images

Boston's Gino Cappelletti scores one of the 24 points he racked up against Buffalo with this extra-point kick in Buffalo, New York, on November 16, 1964. Cappelletti grabbed three touchdown passes and a two-point conversion pass from quarterback Babe Parilli and kicked four other extra points as the Patriots ended Buffalo's nine-game American Football League victory skein 36–28. Parilli (15) holds for Cappelletti, and Buffalo's George Saimes (26) makes a vain attempt to block the kick. AP Photo/LM

Don Maynard, New York Jets end, lands upside down after receiving a pass from quarterback Joe Namath in the first quarter of the game against the Cincinnati Bengals in New York's Shea Stadium, December 8, 1968. The pass was good for a long gain, adding to Maynard's lifetime total of more than 9,300 yards gained, an all-pro record for an end. AP Photo/John Duricka

9

Tall Tales and Short Stories

THEY LIKED IKE

Just call him, "The Wild Man."

Larry Eisenhauer was known not only as one of the greatest defensive ends in Patriots history but also for his bizarre behavior on and off the field.

Always pushing the envelope—and usually somebody else along with it.

"I was always known as a guy that got himself very emotionally motivated before games," says Eisenhauer.

Before going on the field, "Ike" put on his shoulder pads and then a show.

Look out, locker! The metal door rattled as Ike slammed it with all his force again and again. It was Ike's way to get his adrenaline flowing.

That was one way.

On the field before introductions, Ike put on another show.

Like a bull, Ike put his head down and raced 10 feet straight into a goalpost. He did it again.

After several of these shots, opposing players began to cast strange looks toward the Patriots' bench.

Not even the Patriots were safe from his shenanigans. Running as fast as he could, Ike slammed into one of his teammates on the sideline.

The Wild Man was creative—anything to upset the status quo.

And then there was the "jockstrap" incident that teammates love to relate.

It was before a big game in Kansas City late in the season. Eisenhauer left the locker room and walked into the freezing tunnel leading to the field wearing only cleats, socks, jock, and helmet.

"I walked out of the locker room and about halfway up the tunnel to the field. Not all the way, mind you—just halfway."

"Nobody in the stands could see me. It was a big game for us, and I did it just to loosen up everybody. Guys were laughing."

It was just another ordinary day for The Wild Man.

GETTING ALONG SWIMMINGLY

It's a classic Larry Eisenhauer story that has been told and retold through the years. Around the Boston Patriots in the 1960s, it was known as the "Mermaid Story."

The 1963 AFL championship game was being played in San Diego between the Patriots and Chargers. The Boston players were staying at a swanky hotel.

Newspaperman Ron Hobson remembers the scene: "There was a place called the 'Mermaid Bar,' and in back of the bartender was a glass wall and an underground pool."

The mermaid show was scheduled to go on at 9:00. Eisenhauer was planning to put on a show of his own.

Eisenhauer's father had arrived in town to see the game, exhausted from his long trip on the old propeller planes. "Larry's father was a great character, he looked just like Larry except he's a 350-pound guy," Hobson remembers.

Larry's dad was hot and tired from his trip and wanted to cool off.

"Larry says, 'Take a swim, dad. Don't go until after nine because they're putting chlorine in the pool.'"

"Sure, son," Eisenhauer's father said.

"So at nine o'clock, everybody gathers down in the bar, and the mermaid show has started," Hobson noted. "At 9:05, here comes a 350-pound guy, jumps right in the middle of the pool, scattering all the mermaids, their nose pieces flying everywhere. It was hilarious."

In one version of the story, he was followed by his son, the prank-playing Larry Eisenhauer. Patrick Sullivan, son of Patriots owner Billy Sullivan, remembers it well.

"I was summoned to the bar with my father because the manager of the hotel called my father to tell him that one of the players was in the pool with these mermaids," recalled Sullivan. "I was 10 at the time. I immediately said to my dad, 'It's got to be Ike.'

"And when we arrived there, sure enough, there's 'Ike' Eisenhauer in the pool."

In conjunction with the Patriots' fiftieth anniversary in 2010, club spokesman Stacey James told Sullivan that an "All-Character Team" would be named.

"The captain's going to have to be Larry Eisenhauer," James told Sullivan.

THE UN-JET SET

When the New York Jets were playing in the AFL in the 1960s, they were clearly the second-class football team in town. While the Giants were getting first-class treatment by the *New York Times*, the Jets were pretty much flying under the newspaper's radar.

"The *Times* thought so little of the Jets that after Dean McGowan covered them on Saturday, he would take Sunday off," recalled longtime *Times* sportswriter Gerry Eskenazi. "So unless you got the very late edition of Sunday's paper, you wouldn't know what the Jets did."

Eskenazi's assignment on Sunday: write a Jets' follow-up story.

Frank Ramos, the Jets' public relations man, would call Eskenazi with an angle. Win or lose, Ramos would put a positive Jets spin on the game—after all, that was his job.

"The Jets were like a 7–7 team, and yet it would come out in the paper that they were doing great stuff," Eskenazi said.

Eskenazi didn't know much about the game the Jets played that weekend—only what he read in the paper.

"So in a sense, the PR guy was controlling the story for the Jets in the Monday paper. He got me quotes and stuff like that. I never spoke to any of the players.

"It just struck me as so odd that I would be writing about a game I never saw, and more people would be reading my follow-up story in the Monday paper than the original game story. I think the editors felt they should cover something about the game. We weren't really quite sure how to handle it."

MARA OR LESS?

When Joe Namath joined the Jets in 1965, New York newspapers naturally expanded coverage of the team. That led to Wellington Mara's letter to the *New York Times*.

Mara, owner of the New York Giants, fired off a letter to *Times* sports editor Jim Roach. Mara complained that the Jets were getting more coverage in the paper than his team.

Roach dispatched the *Times'* great "numbers nut," Frank Litsky, to do some detective work. He looked at back issues of the *Times* to find out if Mara was right.

"In those days before electronics, we kept every newspaper from every day," remembered Gerry Eskenazi.

"We had the tear sheets in bound volumes. So Roach asked Frank to go back to January 1 that year and measure in inches with a ruler the coverage given to the Giants [as opposed to] the Jets."

Litsky measured every story covering the Jets and Giants. The outcome: Mara was wrong.

"It was actually the Giants who got a little more space," Eskenazi said. "And Roach put that on the bulletin board, with his reply to Mara."

Mara had no answer to that.

WISHFUL THINKING

Harry Wismer, original owner of the New York Titans, had to be one of the most optimistic men in the world.

Before the Titans became the Jets, the Buffalo Bills were in town for a game. Bills owner Ralph Wilson was invited to sit with Wismer in the press box at the Polo Grounds.

As it turned out, only 5,000 people showed up for the game.

Suddenly, a band started to play "Everything's Coming Up Roses." Wismer turned to his wife and said, "Listen, hon, they're playing our song."

The irony wasn't lost on Wilson.

"Here am I in this empty building, and Wismer thinks everything's coming up roses."

WINDED

Jerry Mays of the Kansas City Chiefs remembered an exhibition game in Atlanta when the team bus ran over a water main, negating team showers.

It was bad news for fellow plane travelers.

"We followed Hank Stram's dress code and wore our jackets and ties on the plane ride home, but our faces were covered with mud and sweat, and the stewardesses tried to stay upwind of us for the entire flight," Mays remembered.

WIDE-OUT

Elbert Dubenion was a wide receiver famed for catching the longest pass in AFL playoff history, a 93-yarder thrown by Daryle Lamonica for Buffalo.

He played from 1960 to 1968, and no one had to tell him when it was time to retire.

"I went into the locker room one day," he said," and my locker was cleared out."

HOBBLING ALONG

One of Ron Hobson's many assignments as a young sportswriter for the *Patriot-Ledger* in Quincy, Massachusetts, was to cover the new pro football team in Boston known as the Patriots.

The way he tells it, Hobson had to be nearly as athletic as the players for this assignment. One time the Patriots were playing in Mobile, Alabama, and Hobson had to go through some tricky, cat-like maneuvering to deliver his advance stories to his paper.

Writing the story on deadline was easy—trying to get it in the hands of the Western Union operator after hours presented a little bit of a problem.

"The Western Union office closed down at five o'clock," Hobson remembered.

The Western Union operator lived on the second floor—and Hobson took a most unusual route to get the copy into his hands.

"I had to climb up a ladder on the side of the house, walk across a shed roof, and push the copy under a slightly cracked window," Hobson said.

Oh, where were computers when you needed them? Obviously, still a long way off.

"I'll never forget that as long as I live," Hobson said. "Today, I couldn't climb up a ladder."

RAINED OUT

The Boston Patriots had their share of success in the AFL—also their share of colorful stories.

"The Patriots were the most bizarre of all the American Football League teams at that time," said Ron Hobson.

Case in point:

The Patriots were hosting the Dallas Texans, one of the AFL's strongest teams. The Texans were trailing when they tried a pass on the last play of the game.

But it went incomplete.

"A guy in a raincoat ran into the end zone and knocked the ball away from Chris Burford," Hobson recalled. "They all thought it was [Patriots owner] Billy Sullivan in a raincoat. He had one just like it—a London Fog."

The Man in the Raincoat disappeared into history, cloaked in mystery, and the Patriots held on for a big victory.

TAKING A BOW

One of Joe Namath's great moments early in his AFL career featured a New York Jets victory over a strong Boston Patriots team late in the 1966 season. The Patriots' loss opened the door for the Buffalo Bills to gain a berth in the AFL title game.

Bills owner Ralph Wilson was so thrilled and thankful to Namath that he expressed his joy in a very personal way right on the spot.

Remembered sports writer Ron Hobson, "After the Patriots lost, I went into the Jets' locker room. Wilson, wearing a camel hair coat, got down on his knees and bowed to Namath for beating the Patriots."

The Bills, though, fell short in their bid for a third straight AFL championship. They eventually lost to Kansas City 31–7, and the Chiefs went on to play in the first interleague title game soon to be known as the Super Bowl.

CHARGE!

The San Diego Chargers were one of the early powerhouses of the AFL, advancing to the league championship game five times in the first six years of their existence.

They won only one of those games, though. It was played on January 5, 1964, in Balboa Park, located near the famed San Diego Zoo.

"It didn't sell out," said Ron Hobson, who sat on the roof in a makeshift press box because the small main press box didn't have any room for him. Sitting next to him was none other than Tom Harmon, the great Michigan running back.

"It was well attended and taken very seriously in the Boston media," Hobson recalled of the 1963 championship game. "There were not many TV stations coming out to do it, but we had plenty of guys from the print media."

The Patriots were almost sorry they made the trip, losing 51–10 in one of the worst pro football blowouts in championship history.

"San Diego was a big-time team," Hobson recalled, "and the Patriots got slaughtered."

A GIANT ATTACHMENT

Hard to believe, but once upon a time, the New York Giants were the favored pro football team in New England. In fact, they were the only pro football team with a notable presence.

Before the AFL fielded a team in Boston in 1960, all Giants games were shown on local television, the closest thing approximating a "home" team for New England football fans.

"I was a big Giants fan," remembered Pat Sullivan, son of long-time Patriots owner Billy Sullivan. "The games were blacked out in New York, and we saw every Giants game. You'd see the Giants 12, 14 times a year, depending on how many games were played in that particular year.

"As a kid, I remember distinctly watching the 1958 game [between the Giants and Baltimore Colts for the NFL title] with my father, and he said, 'This is the game of the future, not baseball.'"

Patrick's allegiances changed, of course, as soon as his father became one of the owners of the new Boston Patriots.

HAVING A BALL

The Boston Patriots weren't giving away anything in the early years of their existence—certainly not footballs.

Patrick Sullivan remembers his days as a ball boy when one of his jobs was retrieving footballs from the stands.

"Before we had nets, we used to go up in the stands and try to catch the ball because you'd have a 45–42 game and you'd be kicking a lot of extra points," said Sullivan, son of original Patriots owner Billy Sullivan.

"The ball would go into the stands, and there would be a little scrum in there. We had a group of ball boys, a couple of big hooligans, and then I'd come in, and I was sort of the little guy. I'd grab the ball when it dropped on the ground and run away. That was the drill that we had."

You couldn't blame the Patriots for saving those footballs. Any cost-cutting measure was welcome in those uncertain years.

THE WAITING GAME

Times were financially tight for many teams at the start of the AFL in 1960. One of these teams was the Boston Patriots, who tried to cut corners wherever they could.

By the time Gil Santos joined the Patriots' broadcasting team in 1966, he was well familiar with a legendary team story regarding cost cutting.

The Patriots were scheduled to play a night game in Buffalo and arrived in town the day before so they would be well rested.

The next morning, the day of the game, the Patriots were told they could have the hotel room only until checkout time at 11:00 a.m. Otherwise, the team would have to pay for an extra night.

It was still several hours until game time. What would the team do?

"They convinced the hotel to let them stay as long as they didn't get in the beds or use the room other than to just sit there and wait to go to the game," Santos said. "The day of the game, they were just sitting in chairs in their rooms."

The Patriots were counting on being well rested for the game—but certainly not that well rested.

FOOL ME ONCE

Harry Wismer, a well-known sports announcer who was an original owner of the New York Titans, was a fun-loving guy who enjoyed playing pranks on fellow owners.

One day early in the morning, the phone rang at the home of Patriots owner Billy Sullivan, who was fast asleep.

Sullivan's son, Patrick, answered.

"Where is Billy Sullivan?" the voice at the end said in a demanding voice.

"Who's calling?"

"This is his Eminence, Richard Cardinal Cushing!"

Patrick Sullivan wondered what the Cardinal was doing calling his father at three in the morning.

"Get your old man out of bed. They're running out of oil in Saint Agatha's parish in Dorchester," the nasally voice continued.

Sullivan remembered the phone call in vivid detail.

"I knew my father knew Cushing. My dad ran an oil company, and one of his customers was the archdiocese. So this was not improbable."

So Patrick dragged his father out of bed.

Half asleep, Billy Sullivan put the phone to his ear.

"Your Eminence?"

"Of course, Harry would say, 'It's not his Eminence, it's me, Billy!'"

Wismer also did a pretty good imitation of John F. Kennedy, but when another call later came from the "president" in the wee hours of the morning, Billy Sullivan wasn't the least bit fooled.

BERRY GOOD

Raymond Berry is one of Patrick Sullivan's favorite people. It's easy to see why.

Sullivan, son of original Patriots owner Billy Sullivan, had two memorable encounters with the Baltimore Colts Hall of Famer.

The story begins in 1966, after the AFL had agreed to a merger with the NFL.

"There wasn't interleague play at that point, but we played preseason games against the NFL," Sullivan recalls. "The first preseason game we played against the NFL was against the Colts."

Sullivan, 14 at the time, was helping the visiting clubhouse attendant at Harvard Stadium load the Colts' equipment on a van after the game.

"I don't even remember the outcome of the game," Sullivan said, "but I'm loading the Colts' stuff into their moving van. And this guy stops and looks down and says, 'Let me give you a hand with that, son.'"

It was Raymond Berry.

Sullivan politely refused his offer.

"That was the first of two times in my entire career working in the business, which went from the time I was eight until the time I was 38, that a coach or a player offered to help."

The second time:

"It was in 1978, and we had a big blizzard," Sullivan remembers. "I was 26 years old, and I was managing the stadium in Foxboro. I was driving a front-end loader moving snow out of the parking lot.

"The coaches were coming in to do some work, and I see this guy walking towards me. He walks up next to the front-end loader and says, 'Give me a shovel, I'll give you a hand.' And it's Raymond Berry."

Once again, Sullivan politely turned down Berry's offer to help.

"Chuck Fairbanks was our coach, and if he ever felt that I'd ask one of the coaches to shovel snow, he would have fired me," Sullivan recalled.

Sullivan had a chance to repay Berry for his kindnesses.

In 1984, when Sullivan was the Patriots' general manager, he hired Berry to be his coach.

The next year, Berry took the Patriots to the Super Bowl.

LESSONS FROM DAD

Few pro football owners matched the human touch exhibited by Billy Sullivan of the Boston Patriots.

"He prohibited us from writing form letters," remembered his son, Patrick Sullivan. "So when a season-ticket holder wrote a letter, we had to respond to that letter individually.

"And he wrote between 500 and 1,500 letters a week. There were two secretaries that did nothing but return fan mail.

"My father had this great sense of public relations. It was a different world. He really knew most of the season-ticket holders to the Patriots because, you know, there weren't that many."

As if Billy Sullivan didn't have his hands full enough running an AFL team and writing all those letters, he was given additional duties by NFL commissioner Pete Rozelle once the leagues merged.

Rozelle put the Patriots' owner in charge of both NFL Properties and NFL Films.

Smart move. Sullivan guided those departments of the NFL to new heights.

IN THE MONEY

It doesn't sound like much today, but a $7,500 contract to play pro football for the Buffalo Bills was like hitting the lottery for Ed Rutkowski.

"For a poor kid out of the coal mines of Pennsylvania, that was a lot of money," Rutkowski remembered of his 1963 signing.

Rutkowski, who had played at Notre Dame, also received a $300 bonus.

"I called my mom, and she was all excited," Rutkowski said.

What did he do with his newfound fortune?

"I took $150 out of the bonus to buy my mom a new pair of false teeth. That's what she wanted."

Rutkowski took the other $150 and drove down to Fort Lauderdale for spring break with a bunch of Notre Dame teammates.

"I came back with about $20 in my pocket. I said, Boy this is it, I finally made it."

Rutkowski's principles cost him even more money. Let him tell how: "I was from Kingston, Pennsylvania, about 150 miles up the road from Philadelphia. So I was always a big Eagles fan. And after I had signed with the Bills, I was approached by the Eagles. They offered me an $8,000 signing bonus and a $16,000 contract, and I said, 'I'm sorry, I already signed with the Buffalo Bills.' Put that in today's context: players would just tear up the contract and sign with the other team.

"Hey, I'm from Pennsylvania. In the coal mines, where I grew up, your word and a handshake was better than any kind of contract. I had to honor what I did with the Buffalo Bills."

SOMETHING TO BE THANKFUL FOR

Coach Lou Saban was a father figure to many of the players on the Buffalo Bills. One time, he gave some fatherly advice to Ed Rutkowski, whom he had invited over for Thanksgiving dinner along with Booker Edgerson.

As Rutkowski recalled, "We're sitting around and talking, and Saban said, 'You're going to have a great career with the Buffalo Bills, and you're going to make a lot of money, but don't do something stupid by going out and buying a damn new car.'

"Well, I had just gotten a new 1964 Pontiac Grand Prix. I had it parked in front of his house. So after dinner, he walked us out. I thought, *Please don't come out to the porch.* Sure enough, he came out on the porch.

"If you were standing on the porch, you could see the car on the street, about 20 yards to the left. So I waved good-bye; I walked out to the sidewalk and made a right and went all the way around the block and waited for about 15 minutes. And next to the car were a tree and a mailbox. I hid behind the tree, snuck up behind the mailbox, crept so nobody could see me, got in the car, and drove away."

A HARD PITCH

Buffalo's Jack Kemp was regarded as one of the hardest-throwing quarterbacks in pro football in his time.

The reason: the Bills had given up a late touchdown to the Broncos.

"We were beating them by two or three touchdowns, and there was like three minutes to go," trainer Ed Abramoski recalled. "They scored in the last minute or two, and in the locker room, Lou just went off on the guys:

"'You can't do that. That's where the game is won! You let up. You can never let up. Blah, blah, blah!'

"And he was going on and on, and I was cutting the tape off of Billy Shaw. Billy turns to me and says, 'Eddie, did we win this game?'"

MYSTERY LUNCH

When Lamar Hunt moved his Dallas team to Kansas City in 1963, it was not very popular with Hunt's partners.

"They wanted to move to Chicago or some other major city," recalled Jack Steadman, Hunt's longtime top business executive. "But Lamar and I talked about it. At that time, Kansas City was a major-league city. They had the A's there. We felt we could gain a foothold in Kansas City and build our franchise there."

Kansas City mayor H. Roe Bartle and the city were excited about getting a pro football team, as was the chamber of commerce and the city council.

Other than the mayor, though, no one knew which team was involved.

"We kept that a secret," Steadman said. "We had a season ticket program going in Dallas at the same time."

Steadman spent five months in Kansas City behind the scenes with the mayor, doing undercover work.

"Bartle had an incredible sense of humor," Steadman said. "So if anybody saw Lamar up there, he would refer to him as 'Mr. Lamar.'"

On one occasion, Steadman went to lunch with the mayor at the Kansas City Club. Everyone wanted to know the identity of his mystery guest.

Said Bartle, "That's Jack X—he's an internal revenue agent in town investigating the expense reports of some of our most prominent citizens."

"Anyway, I was 'Jack X' for five months, but I was able to put the deal together."

A NICE FIT

Moving the Dallas Texans to Kansas City naturally required changing the team name. The "Kansas City Texans" just wouldn't make sense, even if it was owner Lamar Hunt's first choice.

It had to be the "Kansas City Chiefs," and there was a good reason for it, explains Jack Steadman, Hunt's top business executive: "We had a naming contest, and we got a lot of suggestions. One of the people worked for Chiefs Van Line, and he had sent in the name "Chiefs." Mayor H. Roe Bartle was a retired Boy Scout executive, and he had developed a part of the Boy Scouts that had become nationally prominent. His nickname was 'The Chief.'"

One more thing: there was a lot of Indian history in the Kansas City area.

"It really fit very, very well," Steadman said. "So we became the Kansas City Chiefs."

BIRTH OF A FOOTBALL FAN

When the Buffalo Bills opened for business in 1960, Ange Coniglio started a strong love affair with the team. So did his wife, Angie.

"I jumped into it with both feet," he says. "Although I was not a season-ticket holder early on, I went to every game, and so did my wife."

That included the times Angie Coniglio was pregnant.

Attending one game late in the 1965 season, she was "eight and three-quarter months pregnant," according to her husband.

As luck would have it, sitting in the row directly in front of her was her obstetrician.

No matter, Angie said.

"If I have this baby, I'm not leaving the game," she told her husband.

Hearing this, the doctor looked up and said, "I'm not, either."

PS: The Bills went on to win the AFL championship that season. Angie gave birth to a daughter on January 7, 1966, after the season was over.

JET SET

On the day that Weeb Ewbank was hired in 1963 to coach the AFL's New York entry, management changed the team name from the Titans to the Jets.

Why the Jets? No, it had nothing to do with the Mets, even though the football team would be playing its games in the baseball team's new stadium.

Here's the story: Sonny Werblin, one of the principal owners, had noted that the world was entering into the space age and that the Mets' stadium was located between two airports, LaGuardia and Idlewild.

"So we became the Jets," said Jets PR man Frank Ramos.

BECOMING GREEN

Long before green became a color associated with the environmentalist movement, it was the choice of uniform color for the New York Jets in the early 1960s. But not the first choice.

"Sonny Werblin was the most active of the five owners, and he really wanted red, white, and blue uniforms," noted Frank Ramos. "And he was so disappointed when the league told him the Boston Patriots have that color scheme and he couldn't have it."

Werblin went back the drawing board.

"Sonny was born on St. Patrick's Day, so the Jets became green and white," Ramos said. "Howard Cosell later on did a famous documentary in which he said it was green because it was 'Sonny, as in money.'"

WAHOO, THAT'S WHO!

First impressions are important in football, as they are anywhere else. Think of linebacker Edward "Wahoo" McDaniel's start with the New York Jets.

The Jets had acquired McDaniel from the Denver Broncos in 1964.

"We had a Saturday night opener versus Denver in Shea in 1964," remembered Frank Ramos. "Wahoo was having a great game that night. Bob Rais, our PA announcer, said to me at half-time, 'What if I said when he does something, 'Tackle by Guess Who?' and the people probably will say, 'WAHOO.' And that is exactly what happened."

The fans had a lot of fun that night with McDaniel's colorful nickname—he made 24 tackles, according to Ramos.

McDaniel's unusual nickname was courtesy of his father, an oil worker who was nicknamed "Big Wahoo."

McDaniel, a Choctaw-Chickasaw Native American born in Oklahoma, lasted only two seasons in New York. Within a few more years, he had moved on to professional wrestling.

"Wahoo McDaniel was one of my favorite players, wild and crazy, outgoing, a really fun, fun guy to play with," said teammate Willie West.

BETTER TO RECEIVE

With wide-open offenses featuring the long pass, football was fun for AFL teams in the 1960s.

Not so much fun if you were a defensive back, though.

"It was tough to play against those offenses," said Willie West, a defensive back who played a season with the NFL's St. Louis Cardinals before hooking up with AFL teams in Buffalo, Denver, New York, and Miami.

The toughest wide receivers to cover in West's opinion? Try the San Diego Chargers' Lance Alworth, Houston's Charlie Hennigan, Miami's Howard Twilley, and Kansas City's Otis Taylor, just to name a few.

"Lance Alworth was one of the top," West said. "His ability was such that he was both fast and quick. He could jump, along with having great hands. It was always difficult to cover him, every play. Of all the attributes, the speed might have been his best weapon. But he could do it all, the complete package.

"Charlie Hennigan was not really fast, but he could catch, and he had the ability to get you out of sync. He had good moves, a thousand moves.

"Howard Twilley was similar with the Dolphins. He had stick-'em on his hands, it seemed. He could catch anything. He was not even as fast as Charlie Hennigan, but he had these moves that could get you to hesitate, and then he'd be open. Otis Taylor was big and fast, and he not only could outrun you but run over you, too."

THE BIG ONE OF THE BIG THREE

Without Lamar Hunt, Bud Adams, and Barron Hilton, safe to say the AFL never would have become a reality.

The three owners had the resources to keep their teams afloat during the rough early days of the league and to help other teams survive as well. Hunt was the original owner of the Dallas Texans, and Adams owned the Houston Oilers and Hilton the Los Angeles Chargers, who after one season moved to San Diego.

There was no question who was the leader of the pack. Once asked how he got involved in the birth of the AFL, Adams replied, "I'm the one with the plane, so I went wherever Lamar went."

A BLAND RESPONSE

Whether playing in Los Angeles or San Diego, the Chargers were one of the top teams in the AFL. When they faced the Houston Oilers, not so much.

The Oilers beat the Chargers in the AFL's first two championship games. Suffice it to say that they were not the most popular team with the San Diego fans when they came to town.

Houston offensive lineman Norm Evans became well acquainted with the fans' dislike of the Oilers when he was a rookie in 1965.

"We were playing in San Diego, and they introduced our offensive team," Evans recalled. "I come running on the field, and the fans all booed."

The fans saved their loudest boos for Oilers quarterback George Blanda.

"When they introduced Blanda, he comes running on the field, and they give him a standing boo ovation—everybody in the stadium was standing and booing."

It didn't seem to bother Blanda, a crusty veteran who had heard boos at home that season as well as on the road. The Oilers were on their way to a miserable 4–10 record.

"George has this great big smile on his face when he got to the sideline, and he said, 'Wow, this is just like home.'"

For a change, the Chargers beat the Oilers 31–14 that day.

MAN OF THE AUER

For trivia-loving fans, and fans of the Miami Dolphins in particular, here's a good one.

Who scored on the first and last play of the Dolphins' first season in 1966?

The answer: Joe Auer.

"He returned the opening kickoff [against the Oakland Raiders] for a 95-yard touchdown," recalled Norm Evans, who played offensive tackle for the Dolphins from 1966 to 1975. "Then we were playing Houston in the last game.

"We had a long completion, and back then you couldn't spike the ball [to stop the clock], so quarterback John Stofa gave a hand signal for a flare pass to Joe. Stofa flipped him the ball, and he scored."

The Dolphins wound up with a 29–28 victory.

Auer lasted only two seasons with the Dolphins, and Evans insists it was because of an incident involving Dolphins star running back Larry Csonka.

"We were at St. Andrews School in Boca Raton, Florida, for training camp. Joe used to drive this dune buggy, and he took Csonka out, and they had a few too many.

"The school was down this long road in the middle of palmetto bushes, with maybe three-quarters of a mile on a straight road and then a sharp left turn into the school. Auer missed the turn and rolled the dune buggy. Csonka landed in the sand and bushes and had a big scrape on his head."

As the story goes, Csonka got scraped, and Auer got cut.

CHARGE IT

A football team named after a credit card? No way, says Barron Hilton.

"Lots of people thought it was because I was running Carte Blanche, but that is not true," says the original owner of the Chargers.

The real scoop on the Chargers' name: "The name was chosen from the USC [University of Southern California] bugle call," Hilton says.

At that time, Hilton's team played its games in the Coliseum, sharing the field with the Southern Cal football team.

The Trojans featured a dramatic entrance at their games by the Southern Cal mascot, a white horse named Traveler. Astride the horse was a Trojan warrior blowing a bugle—a tradition that still exists today.

"We thought it a good name because everybody was yelling 'Charge' at the Coliseum, like pushing a hot button on everybody's tail," Hilton said.

As for the distinctive lightning bolt on the helmet, Hilton said, "I selected the bolts from the Air Force Academy. I love to fly. I used a different bolt than the one at the academy there. Ours was a little more elongated."

LIGHTS OUT

Harry Wismer's financial problems with the New York Titans were well documented around the AFL in the early 1960s. Wismer had all he could do to meet his bills—and very often didn't.

One day the Titans were playing the San Diego Chargers in the Polo Grounds with dark quickly descending in the late afternoon. Recalled linebacker Larry Grantham, "We were ahead in the game by some trick of fate because San Diego was better than us. The referee stopped the game and called time-out to come over and tell our coach to put the lights on.

"But Harry Wismer said, 'Why? We are doing pretty damn good in the dark.'"

They turned on the lights.

"I don't think we won the game, either," Grantham said.

THE MONEY GAME

When the New York Jets signed Joe Namath to an unprecedented $400,000 deal in 1965, it raised the contract level all across the team.

Coach Weeb Ewbank wanted to make sure that the veteran players were happy with their own contracts. Larry Grantham remembered when Ewbank called him and asked how much he wanted.

"I had a one-year contract every year," Grantham relates. "I jacked up my price from what I normally ask for, and he OK'd it on the spot. I think I told it to Joe through the years: 'Thanks for getting me that extra money.'"

Namath's presence on the Jets also helped his teammates financially in other ways.

"He helped all of us get a contract with Puma. We were on TV, and they would pay us to wear these shoes. It was because of Joe. We were still out there to make a living."

A PRETTY TOUGH COOKIE

The hardest running back to bring down in the AFL?

For the Jets' Larry Grantham, it was Cookie Gilchrist, hands down.

"Gilchrist could have played tackle or guard," said Grantham, one of the Jets' all-time great linebackers.

Grantham's "worst moment" in his football life involved the Buffalo running back.

"Cookie was the fullback, and our middle linebacker got hurt, and we tried to disguise an odd-man line and stack me behind the center," Grantham recalled. "I weighed about half of what Cookie weighed."

Gilchrist was unstoppable, even by the Jets' star.

"Cookie ran and ran and ran, and finally they took him out, they were beating us so bad."

But then the Bills realized that Gilchrist was just a few yards short of the record for yards gained in a game.

"I was breathing a sigh of relief," recalled Grantham, "until I look and see they sent him in to get the yardage record."

BLAZING SCOUTS

Before joining the Oakland Raiders in 1969, Al Locasale was a scout for the Chargers, both in Los Angeles and in San Diego.

He liked the job but at first didn't like the blazer he had to wear.

"It was mustard-yellow and it was ghastly," Locasale recalled.

The idea of a blazer for the Chargers' coaching staff came from Esther Gillman, wife of head coach Sid Gillman.

Like it or not, Locasale soon found that the "ghastly" jacket started paying dividends.

"It was one of the things that really helped me. I would call a college coach who was getting ready for the draft to get some information from him. Remember, they are visited by 50 scouts during the year. But they would remember me: 'You are the little guy in the yellow jacket.' Being diminutive and wearing that jacket, I stood out in their memory."

Whenever he visited a college on a scouting mission, Locasale also made it a point to eat in the cafeteria wherever the athletes were eating.

That's where the blazer came into play again.

"I'd eat in the cafeteria they used and was wearing that blazer. They would come up and talk to you, and then they would remember you. By spending so much time around the campus and with the players, it gave me visibility."

The yellow blazer eventually became old fashioned.

"I think we went to something blue that had a very nice embroidered crest that you could put on your jacket pocket, so you'd have the team name sitting on the jacket.

"Recognition was such an important thing."

JUST FINE WITH HIM

Sid Gillman kept tight reins on his players in training camp, particularly when it came to bed check.

Scout Al Locasale remembered when the San Diego Chargers' coach caught a player trying to sneak out for a night on the town.

"One night Sid was making a late-night bed check, and we find a player whose window was up in a ground-level cabin. He was standing there. One foot is inside the window on the floor, the other is on the ground outside the window. The guy looks at Sid and says, 'I am going to get fined, right?'

"Sid said, yeah, and told him if he was just getting back into his room, it would be $500, and it's just $100 if he was stepping out because he had not left yet.

"But Sid laughed it off and fined him the minimum."

REALLY ON A HOT STREAK

Lamar Hunt took pride in his accomplishment as one of the founders of the AFL.

Another source of pride: his wife's attendance record at Super Bowls.

"Any discussion of the Super Bowl, my father has tied back to my mother," noted Lamar's son, Clark. "The [NFL] commissioner has mentioned that she's the only woman and one of the few people to have attended all the Super Bowls.

"In fact, before my father passed away, he called me to his bed. At this point he and she had seen the first 40 Super Bowls that had been played, and he was very proud of her streak of seeing all those games."

Clark Hunt said that his father gave him "a lot of fatherly advice, a lot of it relating to my kids, some of it relating to the Chiefs.

"But one of the most important things he told me that day was to make sure that we got my mother to Super Bowl XLI, which was going to be played only a few weeks later."

Not only did Norma Hunt attend that game, but the NFL commissioner invited her to be part of the coin toss ceremony.

"Since then, she's made Super Bowl XLII and Super Bowl XLIII," Clark Hunt said in an interview at the start of the 2009 season.

Mrs. Hunt adds a private family joke: "Lamar absolutely loved statistics, and for whatever reason it seemed that this Super Bowl streak was something that he just especially loved telling people about. As the years went on and Roman numerals got higher and higher, I said to him, 'Lamar, if you're going to tell everybody in the world that I've seen 40 Super Bowls, I want you to tell them that I was eight when I saw the first one.'"

A LONG WINTER'S NIGHT

Max Winter wasn't the most popular figure in the AFL after making a last-minute jump to the NFL in 1960. In fact, he was seen by many as a traitor.

Winter supposedly was committed and all set to join the AFL with his Minneapolis team. He changed his mind, however, when the NFL offered him a franchise.

The timing couldn't have been worse for the AFL. It came right before the player draft and sent the AFL scrambling to find another franchise to fill the void.

"This was really devastating to Lamar and his fellow owners," said Norma Hunt, Lamar Hunt's widow.

Fast-forward to Super Bowl IV and Hunt's Kansas City Chiefs are playing none other than the Minnesota Vikings, Winter's original NFL team.

It was the second Super Bowl in four years for the Chiefs—they had lost Super Bowl I three years before. Now they hoped to make up for that loss and, not incidentally, square the Super Bowl total at two victories for each league.

"Both Lamar and I were extremely nervous about that game against the Minnesota Vikings," Norma Hunt said. "It was important, too important frankly I'm sure in our own minds, to the history of the Chiefs and the history of the American Football League.

"And, unfortunately, having lost in Super Bowl I, we knew how tremendously devastating it would be to get to that game and lose it. So the heat was really on the Chiefs, and they were tremendous underdogs. We didn't want to experience that bad feeling of losing again."

As the Hunts were leaving the hotel on the elevator, another couple stepped on for the ride down to the lobby: none other than Max Winter and his wife.

"They were the only other people on the elevator as we went down," Norma Hunt recalled. "They were extremely cordial, as were we. But naturally, it was an extremely awkward moment for all of us.

"Personally, I felt there was just terror in all four of our hearts. As we went our separate ways, Lamar looked at me and said, 'You know, they're more scared than we are.'"

Lamar Hunt predicted right then and there to his wife the Chiefs would win—which they did in grand fashion 23–7, tying the Super Bowl score between the leagues 2–2.

"Of all the wonderful memories we shared over all those years at the Super Bowl, I can tell you that there was truly no better feeling in the world than winning Super Bowl IV," Norma Hunt said.

GOING PRO

It's rare when a rookie reporter gets to cover a pro football team in his very first year on the job. So you can imagine how Ron Hobson felt when he was handed the assignment of covering the Patriots in 1960 for the *Quincy (MA) Patriot-Ledger*.

The only problem: it was a team starting out in the new American Football League.

"No one took the AFL seriously," said Hobson.

Indeed, the sports editor of the *Patriot-Ledger* told him at the time that the AFL was "not going to last very long."

Hobson didn't care. He was excited just to be covering pro football.

The league that wasn't supposed to last very long surprised everybody—and Hobson continued to have a long and distinguished career as a sportswriter.

Fifty years later, he was still writing about the Patriots, New England's pride and joy.

ROMANCING THE PRESS

When Sonny Werblin's group bought the New York Titans and changed their name to the Jets in 1963, the team did everything it could to inspire favorable publicity from the press.

This included an extravagant yearly outing starting with a champagne breakfast at the Club 21 that included a three-piece band playing Broadway show tunes.

"Sonny loved the press, loved going to Club 21, loved the New York life, loved to drink, and very quickly got the press behind him with the Jets by catering to us," recalled *Times* sportswriter Gerry Eskenazi.

After breakfast, dozens of reporters and their wives boarded a bus for a day at the Monmouth Park racetrack. Phil Iselin, president of the racetrack, was part of the Jets' new ownership group.

"Betty Iselin, Phil Iselin's wife, would come around with a wicker basket of daily-double tickets and give them out to the spouses of the writers. All the writers were men—and each wife would get a daily-double ticket. In fact, my wife won the daily double one time, a $240 daily double."

The day ended with dinner at a private club. Werblin's wife, Leah Ray, was a band singer in the 1930s, and she would entertain.

"We'd get back about midnight," Eskenazi said. "And that was the day, strictly for the press. It was quite an amazing day."

SHORTCHANGED

Before the age of high-powered agents raking in millions of dollars for their clients, pro football players had to bargain for their own contracts with management.

This put them at an extreme disadvantage.

Sportswriter Ron Hobson recalled when one of the players, Jim Hunt of the Boston Patriots, came to him for advice on his contract in the early 1960s.

"My contract's up, and I'm looking for a raise," he told Hobson. "What do you think is a good raise?"

"Tell me what you make now," Hobson said.

He told Hobson: $12,500.

At that, Hunt was underpaid: the season before, he had an all-pro year and was the team leader in sacks, as Hobson recalled.

"I would think a 20 percent raise would be good—even 30 percent," Hobson told Hunt.

Later that week, Hunt caught Hobson's eye as the Patriots were getting ready for a game.

"Ron, thanks for your help," Hunt said.

"How did you make out?" Hobson asked.

"I got a new deal," the player said, "I got $14,000."

Hobson didn't know what to say. He didn't say anything, but, "You're welcome."

"Geez, just a $1,500 raise after a season like that," Hobson recalled. "But that's the way it was in those days."

RAISING THE STAKES

Players don't usually report to training camp without having signed their contracts. For Ed Rutkowski of the Buffalo Bills, it was purely inadvertent.

"This one off-season, they sent me a contract, and it was a $500 raise," Rutkowski remembered. "I just put it in my desk drawer, and I kind of forgot about it."

Rutkowski went to camp, contract still unsigned.

"We were in there two days. After the afternoon session, Harvey Johnson, the player personnel director, gathered us all together and said there were a couple of guys he wanted to see. I was one of them. I'm thinking, what's all this about?

"He got us into this room and raked us over the coals for trying to demoralize the team by holding out. We all realized that we had forgotten to send our contracts back."

In Rutkowski's words, Johnson gave the players an ultimatum: *I'm going to give you guys a half hour to think about it. You're all going to get a $1,500 raise—take it or leave it, give me your answers.*

When Johnson left the room, the players had all they could do to suppress their glee.

"They only had me down for a $500 raise—so $1,500 I would take in a heartbeat," Rutkowski said. "So we had to find out who was going to go out and tell Harvey without laughing that we would accept his proposal. I came home and told my wife, 'You're not going to believe this, but I just got a $1,500 raise.'"

SHOOTING FOR THE STARS

After three years in the AFL, the New York Titans were in a big hole. Fourth and long, you might say.

So when a new ownership group came in headed by Sonny Werblin in 1963, things didn't look too bright at the outset.

"Our biggest thing was just getting recognized for being viable," Jets publicist Frank Ramos says. "It was Joe Donnelly who wrote for *Newsday* about a Titans game: 'The attendance was announced at 24,000, and 12,000 came disguised as empty seats' in the Polo Grounds.

"The 1962 attendance was something like 36,000 for the entire season. [Owner Harry] Wismer would announce an enormous number of people, and the players would look around and say, 'Where?'"

Enter Sonny Werblin, who had worked for many years in the entertainment industry. A dynamic figure, Werblin was known as "Mr. Show Business" and had a lot of big-name contacts in the industry.

One of the highest-profile personalities at that time was Johnny Carson. Werblin talked the late-night TV talk show host into making an appearance at Jets camp.

"We came up with the idea of having Johnny suit up and play against the Jets, call four plays at the end of practice," says Ramos.

"So Johnny comes, and he ran the plays, and then he showed it on the *Tonight* show. On the last play, it was designed he would get hit, and a bunch of guys would pile on him.

"We were doing everything to get attention. We were probably the first football team on the *Tonight* show."

10

Forcing the Merger

By the end of 1965, the AFL had its sugar daddy in NBC (to the tune of $36 million, not including additional money for playoffs). It had stars both established (Lance Alworth, Jack Kemp, and Nick Buoniconti) and emerging (Joe Namath, Buck Buchanan, and Willie Brown). It rapidly was gaining acceptance from the public.

Now the AFL needed a merger.

Or did it?

Although the AFL and NFL had begun serious talks about a merger, there was a strong belief among some AFL members that it could win a protracted battle with the NFL over talent and survive on its own—or at least gain a position so that any merger would feature settlement terms quite favorable to the AFL.

"I was just trying to lead them in the right direction to get what they wanted, but we could have beaten them," Oakland's Al Davis said, recalling when he served as AFL commissioner in 1966, just before serious merger talks began. "I didn't necessarily want a merger, but they wanted it. And they got it.

"I'll tell you this, [the AFL owners] were sitting in Sonny Werblin's house having a meeting. We didn't know if the National Football League was on the level or joking."

Said one of the owners, "If they're lying to us, we'll have to drop the bomb on them!"

The meaning was clear, according to Davis: "We would drop the bomb and sign all of their players."

Werblin was turning the terrible Titans into the rising Jets. He also wanted no part of a merger. He figured he was in a big city and was having success after moving the franchise from the dilapidated Polo Grounds into a brand new Shea Stadium in 1964, then signing Namath.

Werblin even was outmaneuvering the Giants for some New York fans, so why did he need to pay his way into the big time?

"People forget what an incredible dynamo he was," Jets publicist Frank Ramos said. "When he retired from show business when he left from MCA, the front page of *Variety* read, 'Mr. Show Business Retires.' That is how important he was and how much he really knew about the business.

"Sonny understood how to popularize something. Right off the bat in 1963 when he took over the franchise, our offices were at 57th and Madison in the Fuller Building, a famous [Manhattan] art gallery building. We put our logos across the building, and when someone asked why there, Sonny said, 'This is the fourth-busiest corner in the world.' *In the world*, if you can imagine."

When the fall clothing season was coming up, the Jets introduced themselves to the top New York department stores and asked for their help in promoting football.

"We went out to all these stores in Manhattan in June and July," Ramos said. "We even did it in Saks and Bloomingdale's. We called on these people and put things like footballs and shoulder pads and helmets and giant photos of Jets players in their displays. Who knew Larry Grantham or Don Maynard at that time? These stores didn't care what team; all they cared was the football and fall motif that worked so well together. For these same stores, the Giants couldn't be bothered when they called them to ask to take part."

The AFL was doing well enough in the competition for draft picks and veterans that powerful men such as Davis and Werblin could have been quite persuasive. But for all the strides Werblin was making and for all the popularity of some of the other franchises in their home bases—San Diego, Kansas City, and Houston were about to get new, substantially upgraded stadiums, which New York already had—it remained clear that the NFL still had the upper hand in most every way.

More TV money. Deep-pocketed owners in nearly every city. Tradition.

"The merger was not needed on our side [at that time]; it was desired," said Art Modell, then owner of the Browns, one of the NFL's premier franchises. "We could have done our business for another 30 years. We sought it out to prolong the success of pro football before things got out of hand and we couldn't control them. But there was some animosity."

Even as the two leagues were ravaging each other with escalating price tags on players, the AFL and NFL consented to merger talks.

Actually, informal talks had begun long before things got serious in 1965 and 1966. They even involved the likes of Werblin, despite his insistence that New York could be a two-team, two-league football town.

Ralph Wilson was involved in some of those talks in the days before his Bills would be raided for a key player, and he would become a staunch advocate of an eye-for-an-eye approach.

"When Barron Hilton was president of the AFL, there were some rumors floating, but we never thought we were ever going to have any merger," Wilson said. "We didn't go in it for that. I went in it because I liked football.

"But there were rumors that the NFL was going to be interested in talking about a merger. So they appointed [Colts owner] Carroll Rosenbloom, and Barron appointed Sonny and myself from the AFL to talk. I had a home in Miami, and Carroll had a home in Miami Beach, so I must have met with him 10 times. And it was Carroll who set up the parameters of how this thing would be accomplished because there was a lot of animosity between the leagues."

No kidding! Particularly when NFL commissioner Pete Rozelle instructed Rosenbloom to demand $50 million in indemnity payments by the AFL before a merger could occur.

The enmity then flew into the stratosphere like one of Pete Gogolak's majestic field goals when the Buffalo placekicker—who as the first significant soccer-style kicker in pro football revolutionized the game—played out his contract with the Bills.

With free agency decades away, Gogolak normally would have had few options. He could have held out for more money from the Bills, requested and been granted a trade, or retired.

Ah, but there was somewhere else he could go: the NFL.

ANGE CONIGLIO

Ange Coniglio, super fan.

Uh, better make that super-duper fan.

"What I am," says the Buffalo native, "is an undying American Football League fan. I am unabashedly biased."

In his memorabilia collection, Coniglio sports two stadium seats from old War Memorial Stadium with the old Bills logo on one side and the AFL on the other.

And football cards from the 1960s, six or seven scrapbooks with clippings and autographs—tons of autographs.

In his collection, Coniglio also has personal letters from Lamar Hunt and every other owner involved in the original AFL.

So you can see that Coniglio is a fan, but hardly an average one.

He has maintained his own AFL website, RemembertheAFL .com, not only as a tribute to the old league but a constant source of information for fans and players alike. Coniglio boasts that he has 700 e-mail addresses of AFL fans and 300 of AFL players.

He is continually in touch with many of them, keeping them abreast of news regarding the AFL.

Coniglio goes back to day 1 of the Bills—actually, even before that when his sisters took him to games in the old All-America Football Conference (AAFC). Buffalo had an entry in the AAFC.

"I was just a child then, but that was the start of my rocky relationship with the National Football League," says Coniglio, a retired civil engineer and university professor.

When that league folded, citizens of Buffalo put up a public bond and raised enough money for a franchise in the NFL. The NFL ignored that and disbanded the AAFC and picked up the best players. The NFL kept three teams—Baltimore, San Francisco, and Cleveland.

A few years after that, when the AFL came to town, Coniglio "jumped into it with both feet. Although I was not a season ticket holder early on, I went to every game and so did my wife."

Coniglio noted that the crowds were very good at Bills games, even though the team wasn't very good.

"But they had some great talent in the league. Let me put it this way: I never thought I was watching minor league football watching the AFL. Even in the early years, they had Billy Cannon, Abner Haynes, Jim Otto."

Coniglio remembered when he first heard of the merger between the NFL and AFL. It was June 1966, and Coniglio and his wife were driving to visit his sister in Illinois. They heard the report of the merger on the radio.

"From that instant, I wanted the AFL to remain the AFL," Coniglio said.

He started writing letters and lobbying, pleading to keep the name of the AFL. No luck.

Coniglio had lost his battle to maintain a two-league system, like the American and National leagues in baseball.

"The rivalry between the leagues was tremendous. Hatred is a good thing when it comes to sports. What's better than the Yankees–Red Sox? And that's the way it was between the AFL and NFL.

"When the Jets won that Super Bowl [in January 1969], I couldn't have been happier if the Bills had won it. And that's another theme you'll see in the letters to my website. I mean, it was *our* team."

When the Jets played their first game in Buffalo after the 1969 season, a large group of Buffalo fans met the Jets at the airport and cheered when they got off the plane.

"When they came out on the field, they had a standing ovation from the Buffalo fans," Coniglio recalls. "When are you ever going to see a rivalry like AFL-NFL again?"

Or was there?

According to Dallas Cowboys president Tex Schramm, a major power broker in the NFL who also was a behind-the-scenes participant in early merger talks, his peers and their AFL counterparts had a tacit agreement not to touch players in Gogolak's position. He was an AFL problem, an NFL untouchable.

Then the Giants signed him for $32,000 a year for three seasons.

"That nearly destroyed the merger talks," Schramm said, disputing the theory that it actually was a catalyst for peace. "What [Giants owner] Wellington Mara did was completely legal, but it also was a big thorn in any negotiations. It caused so much animosity that even some of the owners who had been most eager and cooperative about a merger—such as Ralph—turned the other way.

"We'd had some, I wouldn't call them fruitful talks, but some positive discussions, and the Gogolak thing ended those pretty quickly for a while."

Mara had to persuade his fellow owners that signing Gogolak was no crime, and several prominent NFL executives, including founding father George Halas of the Bears, were angered by the transaction they viewed as more of a transgression.

Davis loved it.

"We came into 1966, and Lamar [Hunt] was working on a deal with Tex," Davis recalled. "Meanwhile, they named me commissioner, and I was in Ralph's office in Detroit. Someone came in and said, 'Ralph, the New York Giants just signed Pete Gogolak.'

"I turned to Ralph and said, 'We've just got ourselves a merger.'"

Or at least the means toward one.

Davis had a plan, and, considering the football genius the man would become, no one should have been surprised that it would work—brilliantly.

Remembered Al Locasale, who worked in the front offices of the Chargers, Raiders, and Bengals? "Al turned to me and said, 'Guys, they just gave us the blueprint for a merger. Now we can go after their guys. We are going after their quarterbacks, after places they feel it.'

"We signed some of them to future contracts, which made NFL clubs realize some of their players who were around then will not be with them for long and would be in the AFL in the future. This forced a serious approach to the merger because they didn't want to or couldn't afford to lose those players."

The AFL had put together a war chest for just such an occasion, and Davis made sure they targeted the quarterbacks. Never mind that in Kemp, Daryle Lamonica, George Blanda, John Hadl, Len Dawson, and, soon, Namath, the AFL already was loaded at the position.

Rams quarterback Roman Gabriel signed a contract that would begin in 1967 and immediately received a $100,000 bonus. Fran Tarkenton and Sonny Jurgensen, future Hall of Famers, were approached. So were solid NFL passers such as Milt Plum.

And then there was the John Brodie case.

No player made out better from the hatefulness on display in the AFL and NFL than the 49ers quarterback. Brodie would turn 31 before the 1966 schedule began. He was in his prime and had a cannon arm and a gambler's intuition. He would fit perfectly in the AFL, with Houston as the projected landing spot.

The previous season, Brodie topped the NFL in completions, yardage, completion percentage, and, most significantly, touchdown passes with 30. His asking price to the Niners was a $65,000 raise.

Davis had dispatched personnel executive extraordinaire Don Klosterman to negotiate with Brodie, but there was virtually no small talk. Klosterman simply handed Brodie an offer of $750,000 for five seasons, with the money paid out over 10 years.

Brodie was flabbergasted. And thrilled, naturally.

He never did sign the deal, though. First, he went back to the 49ers to see if they would match the extravagance displayed by the AFL. Then, with word that a merger could be close, Brodie backed off completely on advice of his lawyers.

Eventually, he threatened a lawsuit and, with a merger agreement in place, wound up with a $921,000 contract with the 49ers over 12 years, plus $75,000 in lawyers' fees.

Houston owner Bud Adams hit Halas hard when he signed a futures contract with Mike Ditka, who merely was the face of the Chicago franchise and possibly the greatest tight end the game has seen.

"They were scared to death in the other league of Bud," Davis said, "because he beat them on Billy Cannon. So they knew he could beat them on Ditka and anybody else."

Davis knew how combative Adams could be. At the Houston owners meetings in 1966 when he was elevated to commissioner after Joe Foss resigned, Davis broke up a fight between Adams and a Houston sportswriter, Jack Gallagher. Several AFL owners joked that it was the first and last time Al Davis served the cause of peace.

Schramm even described a bidding competition between NFL teams: Dallas and Green Bay, over Illinois fullback Jim Grabowski.

"We wanted him very badly," Schramm noted. "In those days, you would sign players before the draft, then make a show of taking them, even if you had a guy who was worth a fourth-round pick as your top pick.

"We were signing 95 percent of the guys we wanted, but Green Bay had more cash available and outbid us for Grabowski.

"I decided right there that we had to end this thing."

So, by this point, leaders on both sides—Davis withstanding, perhaps—were sensing the senselessness of it all. The AFL was not about to fold. None of its franchises, not even the financially strapped teams in Boston or Denver, was about to disappear. In fact, the league was about to grow, with an expansion team in Miami beginning play in 1966.

And, according to Gil Brandt, who was in the trenches signing players as personnel director for the Cowboys, the AFL simply was doing a better all-around job than many NFL clubs.

"It was harder for certain people, like Tex, who realized you had to be competitive," Brandt recalled. "A lot of owners in the league said, 'We are the NFL, and we don't have to worry about anything.' What they soon found out is the AFL was making big inroads, especially the teams that had money and were willing to spend it, like Kansas City.

"Finally, what the NFL people found out was that we had better start being aware of all this stuff. Honestly, in the early years the AFL just outworked the NFL teams and got their foothold and took it from there.

"Next thing you knew, they were talking merger."

Doing lots of talking.

"The success of that merger was first effected by Tex Schramm on our side and several of those men on the AFL's side: Ralph Wilson, Lamar Hunt," Art Modell said. "I never thought we would get that far, actually. There was some tremendous opposition on our side against the AFL; I didn't share those feelings. I thought they were a good league and had good names among players, coaches, and owners. They were well-coached teams. I believed it would be nice to get together and merge for the good of pro football."

For the good of pro football.

Even as player raids were grabbing the headlines, the most important negotiations were not with those who played the game but between those who were running it in their respective leagues. Said Schramm, "After the 1965 season, I was convinced the structure of pro football was in trouble. Teams in both leagues were no longer drafting the best players. The draft became predicated on which players you could sign."

With Davis instigating the signing of veterans away from NFL rosters, the clandestine conversations between representatives from both sides grew more intense, with far more urgency to reach an agreement.

Oddly, it seemed that Rozelle wasn't any more keen on a merger than Davis until he realized it was inevitable, that too many team owners on both sides wanted it.

"No question there was animosity," said Joe Browne, Rozelle's chief assistant for much of the commissioner's tenure. "Initially, the NFL owners did not want to merge. They were forced into it by the economics.

"Once the AFL teams showed they were going to spend money for players and the NFL owners realized Bud and Lamar and Ralph and the others were spending, they understood there would be a number of NFL teams—teams in both leagues—that would not be able to afford the competition."

Yet it was several of the more affluent teams that were at the forefront (secretly, of course) of the merger talks: Hunt and the Chiefs, Hilton and the Chargers, and Schramm and the Cowboys.

Hunt and Schramm had a mutual respect from their backgrounds as Texans and from Hunt's willingness to move out of the Dallas market in 1963 for Kansas City, thus not forcing the Cowboys to share a budding market that just might have supported two franchises over the long haul.

They also had a strong desire to end what had gone from occasional skirmishes to a full-out bidding war. As businessmen, each knew how such tactics could weaken or destroy too many members on both sides. As football men, they understood that the sport's growth depended on a peaceful resolution.

Now.

The two powerful Texans had met in Schramm's automobile at a Dallas airport because they feared that actually getting together in the Love Field terminal would draw some attention.

"I was cautiously optimistic," Hunt said. "But these conversations had gone on informally for a number of years, even as early as 1960. I had no reason to think these were going to be any more productive than the ones before."

Schramm believed that some strong groundwork had been laid by those talks between Rosenbloom and Wilson and Werblin and select others. He also knew that Hunt was honorable, reliable, and intelligent enough to recognize the plight both leagues faced.

"Lamar would be honest with you about his feelings and would disagree on some issues, but he would never make a decision in his best interests if it hurt the other [AFL] teams," Schramm said. "He wanted what was best for [pro] football, and I think he understood we wanted the same thing."

Schramm, for his part, was Rozelle's most trusted confidant on major NFL topics. Hunt always would emphasize Schramm's role in the merger.

"He made so many contributions, you would run out of ink if you tried to write them all down," Hunt said.

Paul Tagliabue, who worked as the NFL's chief counsel before replacing Rozelle in 1989, noted, "Pete deployed Tex often. He would emphasize that Tex didn't have many losses on his record."

Hunt and Schramm knew both sides could lose if a merger agreement couldn't be hammered out before the start of the 1966 season.

By the spring of 1966, the asking price—extortion price, if you ask Davis—that the NFL was seeking from AFL teams had dropped precipitously. It had slipped from $50 million to about $18 million over 20 years, or $2 million per club because the Dolphins had joined the AFL ranks.

In addition, the NFL no longer was looking to keep just the solid franchises such as Hunt's and Adams's and Hilton's, fold some others, and even move some. No longer was the NFL insisting that the Jets get out of New York and that the Raiders leave the Bay Area—although Davis would do exactly that decades later.

Even when Gogolak was pirated by the Giants, the talks never collapsed. But there were dicey moments.

Werblin, for example, was so livid about making any payments to the NFL that he was ready to lead an insurrection within the AFL. Cooler heads talked him out of it, even though Werblin, with Namath on board, believed the Jets soon would surpass the Giants in popularity throughout the New York metropolitan area.

"Sonny Werblin was certain we were going to own New York," Namath said. "We had a new stadium [Shea], good young players, and the fans were really taking to us."

Davis also fought such terms of an agreement that gave the NFL any money.

"I remember when the merger came about, how upset Al was that the owners agreed we were paying money to come into the NFL," Locasale said. "He said, 'That's bull, they should be paying us to add our teams to their league to give them life and vitality.' He was very upset because we had established ourselves."

There also was the expansion dilemma. The AFL was heading into Miami, and several other cities were showing interest: Cincinnati, Seattle, and New Orleans. The NFL got the Saints, though, while the Bengals would land in Cincinnati in 1968 with the AFL.

The merger presented other complications, such as scheduling, realignment, selecting a commissioner to suit all, and gaining an antitrust exemption from the government.

Scheduling.

When would AFL and NFL teams play each other?

Some AFL owners were eager for immediate matchups in 1967, the first possible season they could occur. But too many complications existed, most notably the television contracts. And it would be 1970 before regular-season games took place between the AFL clubs, which would become part of the American Football Conference, and the NFL teams (National Football Conference).

But preseason contests would be staged in 1967.

"Sonny said, 'You can't play regular-season games, but we can play four years of preseason games, and then in whatever, 1970, we can have a total merger of the two leagues,'" Wilson recalled. "By then, maybe the animosities would subside.

"So, I said, 'Okay. It sounds all right to me.' But the important thing was we would pool all the TV money."

Realignment.

A very contentious subject.

Most NFL owners sought to keep the setup that would exist when common games began in 1970. That meant 16 teams in the NFL, 10 in the AFL.

It might have gone that way, too, if not for one of the most respected men in football annals—a man who made his reputation first in an earlier rival to the NFL, the All-America Football Conference (AAFC), and then within the NFL itself: Paul Brown.

The leader of the Cleveland Browns when they dominated the AAFC and then entered the NFL and immediately became champions of the established league, Brown had been fired in 1963 by Modell. Five years later, he resurfaced as owner and coach of the Bengals.

With the merger agreement already in place when Brown got the Cincinnati franchise, it was entirely possible that the 16–10 lineup

JON MORRIS

Morris, the Boston Patriots' all-star center, was named to the Patriots' 1960s all-decade team. Morris, a product of Holy Cross, was a two-time AFL all-star and selected for the Pro Bowl five times. The Pats' rookie of the year in 1964, Morris was one of the most durable players in team history. Morris played 11 seasons with the Patriots organization, appearing in 130 games, before joining the Detroit Lions for three years and then the Chicago Bears for his final season in 1978. Following retirement from football, Morris owned a fruit brokerage business in Boston for 30 years.

I was drafted in 1964 in the second round by the Green Bay Packers and in the fourth round by the Patriots, and I used that leverage to bargain for a contract. We didn't have agents in those days. My father and my uncle helped me. We talked with both teams for about three months back and forth, back and forth, until we finally drove the price up to where we thought it wouldn't go any farther. And so I signed with the Patriots. The headline in the old *Boston Traveler* was, "Patriots Sign Holy Cross Rookie to Record Amount." It was a $10,000 bonus and a two-year contract which was guaranteed, which in those days they didn't do. The first year was $13,000, and the second year was $17,000. There just wasn't much money [for football] around in those days. It wasn't until TV exploded that the players were paid decent money.

I always wonder how different my life would have been if I had signed with the Packers. But I don't look back with any regrets because I went to school in New England, I went to Holy Cross, and I love the New England area, and I wanted to stay in the Boston area. I had no desire to live in Green Bay, Wisconsin. I also wanted to go to law school, and I wanted to be in a city where I had the opportunity to do something after football. And so those were all the reasons I signed with the Patriots. And it wasn't the money because the two offers were identical. It was more quality of living and opportunities after football.

Looking back on my career, it was fun. I always remember the coaches saying, "Enjoy it while you can, boys, enjoy all the attention, all the people asking you for your autographs, because once you quit playing, they'll forget about you." Well, they don't. That's not true. Even today, people still say, "Oh, yeah, you're the football player." I get a kick out of that.

The most important game for the American Football League, of course, was the Colts–Jets game, Super Bowl III. I'll never forget the day because we still had this feeling that as AFL players, the National Football League was looking down their noses at us . . . that we weren't as good as they were, and even some of the public was thinking that the NFL was a superior league. We did have a bit of an inferiority complex because of that.

I remember like it was yesterday . . . I was sitting in my house watching the Super Bowl, where Namath [guaranteed the win], and I felt like I was in that game, like I had played, because this game was for all of us. And it turned things around. I think that any AFL player that you talk to, they will tell you that [the Jets–Colts game] was the most important football game for the league.

When the leagues merged, I remember a sense of satisfaction more than anything else for all of us. We had struggled with the AFL being recognized as a major league and always felt that people were wondering about us. It was a tremendous feeling of satisfaction that the merger took place. Now the NFL knows we are as good as they are, and now we're part of the family.

would be kept. Brown saw to it that something more equitable would happen, pushing the other owners to divide the 26 teams into two conferences of 13 each.

Indeed, certain franchises were sure to remain put: the Giants, Bears, 49ers, and Rams. Others were more amenable to a switch, under the right circumstances.

"For competitive balance, and we were interested in seeing pro football survive and prosper, this was the surest way," the Browns' Modell said of the 13–13 split. "I had a feeling of parity with all the teams.

"It was my idea, my willingness to move, and I asked Pittsburgh to go with me because the Steelers were critically important to the Browns, as were the Browns to them.

"Carroll Rosenbloom owned the Colts, and Carroll did things on his own behind the scenes. But I said I would not make the move without [Steelers owner] Art Rooney saying he would go with me."

Modell had been hospitalized for internal bleeding, and Rooney came up to the room with his son, Dan. Modell got the impression that Dan Rooney wasn't thrilled by the idea.

"But Chief chomped on a cigar," Modell said of the elder Rooney, "and said he was going with me. And the rest is history."

Not quite. Modell wouldn't move unless Mara gave him the okay, too, because the Browns and Giants had developed one of the best rivalries in all of sports.

Mara also was in the hospital room and told Modell that he could count on the Giants' support. Mara even agreed to play one pre-season game with the Browns "forever."

Thus, the Colts, Browns, and Steelers headed to the newly formed American Football Conference.

"It wasn't really a merger; it was more of an absorption of the AFL," Modell said. "They had some good franchises in some good cities that would benefit the NFL by bringing them in."

The commissioner.

Davis wanted the job but had no chance. Throughout negotiations, the NFL insisted that Rozelle would be in charge once a merger occurred.

"I think Al would have been a great pick to be the commissioner," Locasale said. "But they went obviously with their guy and built that into the merger package. Al would have been a superb commissioner."

Instead, Davis became a superb owner, and his Raiders would win three Super Bowls. Rozelle, meanwhile, built the NFL into the most popular and prosperous sports league America has known.

"From 1964 to 1966, the NFL did everything we could to devalue the AFL," NFL executive Joe Browne said. "And then we embraced them as part of the merger. In 1966, when we agreed to merge, Pete said that any way we could publicize the AFL was good for us."

Antitrust exemption.

To complete the merger, the leagues needed permission from Congress in the form of an antitrust exemption. They got it with something of a power play.

"When we went to Congress for the antitrust exemption, they asked us why," Browne recalled, "and we explained if you do not do it, franchises would fall by the wayside. Do you want your franchise to be the one that disappears?

"That's when the congressmen realized we should do this, that a merger made sense."

Peace was at hand.

Yet some key AFL people knew they would miss the competition with the NFL.

"It was exciting, it was provocative," Davis told the Associated Press. "But you can tell just by talking to me, I knew we'd beat them. They were scared of us. But things worked out."

Yes, the "little league that could" did.

11

The Super Bowl

Super Bowl? The first champion-
ship game between the NFL and AFL champions didn't have such a
lofty name. It didn't even have any hype.

By today's standards, the AFL-NFL Championship Game in Los
Angeles had all the cachet of a Pro Bowl. Nearly everyone in the NFL,
starting with commissioner Pete Rozelle, didn't really want the game
to take place—what did the established league have to gain? The
stands at the Los Angeles Coliseum weren't even full. Several Green
Bay Packers took the contest so seriously that they spent the week
partying as much as practicing, particularly on the eve of the game.

But the game between the Packers of the NFL and the Kansas City
Chiefs of the AFL was an essential step toward unification of the two
leagues. No merger agreement could have come without it.

"In 1965 or early '66, Pete was not at the top of the list of people who wanted to merge," said Joe Browne, the longtime com-
munications director of the NFL and right-hand man to three
commissioners.

Former Kansas City Chiefs executive Jack Steadman said Rozelle
"really fought" the idea of a title game between the two leagues.

"He just didn't think it was right at all, and he continued to call it
the 'World Championship Game.'"

With much sarcasm, apparently.

Still, Rozelle was a brilliant leader with the sharpest of marketing minds. He clearly understood that once the feuding owners from the two leagues reached a peace treaty, the AFL was part of his football family.

"We went from doing everything we could publicizing the differences between the NFL and the AFL teams to building up the AFL for when we would play preseason games and then regular-season games," Browne noted.

Not to mention championship games.

While Rozelle wasn't thrilled about a title game between the two leagues, he recognized the necessity, knowing that the viability of the merger depended on an ultimate matchup between the NFL and AFL champions. So he appointed a committee on which he served along with the Cowboys' Tex Schramm, the Colts' Carroll Rosenbloom, the Rams' Dan Reeves, and—in the true spirit of compromise that in some ways defined Rozelle's regime—the Chiefs' Lamar Hunt, the Patriots' Billy Sullivan, and the Bills' Ralph Wilson.

Hunt once noted that Rozelle wasn't simply including three AFL owners for balance on the committee that would organize the game. He was "showing us in the AFL that we would be decision makers for the future of the combined leagues. He was showing faith in us as partners in the NFL."

Strange bedfellows, perhaps, but still partners.

While the AFL and NFL would not play common schedules until 1970, the committee had only a few months to organize the title contest. When and where became critical elements.

Just six weeks before the scheduled date of the title game, the NFL decided to stage it in Los Angeles, where the Coliseum, originally built for the 1932 Summer Olympics, could hold 95,000 football fans. Little did anyone know that one-third of the cavernous stadium would be empty for the game.

Hunt suggested a two-week break between the league title games and the big showdown. It was a prescient idea that in future years would be a key to the hoopla surrounding what the Super Bowl would become. It was one of many contributions Hunt made to the Super Bowl, including the name.

Hunt had spotted his daughter, Sharron, playing with a toy ball called a "Super Ball." It was on his mind when the planning committee gathered to talk about the championship game between the two leagues.

During the course of conversation, Hunt jokingly made reference to the game as "the Super Bowl."

"It just came out," said Hunt, adding that he never actually suggested applying the name to the game.

While it took years for Rozelle to accept that monicker, the media loved it from the beginning—even if it wasn't until the Colts–Jets matchup in 1969 that the NFL adopted it. By 1971, the leagues were fully commingled, and the Super Bowl was carrying Roman numerals.

For the title game to earn its place alongside the World Series—baseball still was king in America—it needed some sort of hook, some kind of controversy. The matchup between the Packers and Chiefs on January 15, 1967, generally considered a mismatch, wouldn't do it alone.

Fortunately for Rozelle, Hunt, and everyone else in pro football, television provided that angle.

NBC's contract with the AFL in 1965 provided the lifeblood for the league continuing to compete with the NFL. CBS had the same deal with the NFL.

NBC and CBS were at odds: which network would broadcast the game?

Neither would back down, causing Rozelle much consternation and forcing a significant compromise.

"Television had become very important as far as the league was concerned," Steadman recalled.

In fact, both networks broadcast the game.

"Pete, of course, knew better than anyone the power of TV," Browne said. "He knew that as well as anyone, not just in sports but anyone."

The competition to draw viewers was the most intense part of the buildup to the game, which would feature Hunt's Chiefs—how fitting considering the man's role in creating and nurturing the AFL. The Chiefs would face Vince Lombardi's Packers—again, how fitting that the NFL's dominators of the decade would be the representative.

CBS was awarded the right to provide the video feed for the game, and it spent about $1 million on promotion, a huge amount in those days. NBC spent just as freely.

Rozelle loved the attention pro football was garnering on the airwaves. NBC's duo of play-by-play announcer Curt Gowdy and analyst Paul Christman were trotted out on the *Today* and the *Tonight* shows. CBS made lead announcer Ray Scott and top analyst Frank Gifford, one of the game's most popular figures as a player and then as a TV personality, just as available on its shows.

"You could turn on the television and hear about this game almost everywhere you tuned in on both networks," Hunt said. "It was tremendous publicity."

It was, after all, a first. But would it be remotely competitive?

Most of America didn't believe so. The Packers were 14-point favorites, and the number might have been higher had Green Bay not struggled to beat Dallas 34–27 for the NFL crown. Kansas City routed the Bills 31–7—at Buffalo, no less.

It didn't matter in most football minds—at least those outside the AFL.

"When we came out, the AFL was the stupid stepchild of professional football, and the NFL at that time was bad-mouthing it, saying how it was bad for football," Chiefs quarterback Len Dawson said. "It took a couple of years to say to ourselves, 'Why is it bad? More jobs for players? More jobs for coaches and other people who make up a football team?'"

Dawson did have a comrade in Packers quarterback Bart Starr, whose résumé was far more accomplished by January 1967 but who was an admirer of his counterpart and of the AFL champions.

"One thing I was disappointed about was that the Chiefs were never given their due credit in that first Super Bowl," Starr said. "We recognized when we were preparing for the game just how good they were. Players and coaches knew, and, just a few short years later, they had their moment in the sun when they beat Minnesota in Super Bowl IV."

They'd even have a few moments in the spotlight—just a few—during the buildup to the game with the Packers.

"I remember having the party when the Packers came in to play Kansas City," original Chargers owner Barron Hilton recalled. "It was not the Super Bowl at that time, not what it would become. I had the USC [University of Southern California] Marching Band at the party at the Beverly Hilton, but it was not very [festive]. There was still a lot of hard feelings because of the [bidding] war that had taken place."

Lombardi wasn't letting on if he carried those same harsh feelings. But he fully understood the precarious position the Packers were in. The entire pro football establishment, from commissioner Rozelle to the ball boys in Green Bay, were counting on the Pack to uphold the NFL's reputation. And, as Starr admitted, the Packers knew the Chiefs would be no pushover.

So Lombardi the martinet pushed his team even harder. He had no choice.

"He wasn't really nervous," Starr said. "He was just trying to let us know we were representing the prestige of the NFL. There was great pride. He didn't want us to take that for granted. We were the league's first representative in that game."

As such, the Packers not only needed to win but also needed to win convincingly. Otherwise, all those claims of superiority would become laughable.

Also laughable was the thought that veteran receiver Max McGee, who already was talking about retirement, would play a critical role in the first Super Bowl.

A backup who had all of four receptions during the regular season, McGee was sure he wouldn't be used against Kansas City—so sure that, as was his wont even when he was a starter, he spent much of the previous night and early morning hours partying. Heavy partying.

At that point, the 34-year-old McGee claimed that he held the record for breaking curfew: 11 straight nights. This championship game would be no reason to readjust his schedule.

When McGee showed up in the Packers' dressing room, he told Boyd Dowler, Green Bay's top wideout, "Boy, don't get hurt today. I don't know if I can play."

Then Dowler injured his shoulder early in the first quarter. Suddenly, Lombardi was screaming McGee's name and ordering him onto the field.

"I could barely see where I was going. Playing football is no way to get rid of a hangover," McGee said.

Either McGee was exaggerating or his recuperative powers were legendary. Quickly, the Packers moved into Chiefs territory, and McGee caught Starr's pass for a 37-yard score.

It was hardly a routine completion, either. McGee had to reach back, turning his body awkwardly, to snare the pass. He did, never breaking stride and heading into the end zone for the first score in an AFL-NFL game.

The Chiefs showed their resolve by tying it on Dawson's seven-yard pass to Curtis McClinton. After the Packers got another touchdown, Mike Mercer's field goal made it 14–10 at halftime.

In the stands, in the press box, and everywhere else NFL people congregated, there were sweaty palms and visions of disaster. Stram confidently told his players in the locker room that they were going to win.

Imagine the gloom and doom NFL folks would have felt and the jubilation for AFL followers had that occurred. But McGee, presumably a bit more sober by the second half, and the Packers' defense were dominant.

Plus, Green Bay hammered "The Hammer," Chiefs defensive back Fred Williamson. Known for his crunching tackles and forearm shivers, many of them bordering on assault, Williamson—who later became a movie star—spent much of the buildup and part of the game taunting the Packers.

Late in the game, the Packers ran the ball.

"I remember the play," Williamson said. "I knocked Fuzzy Thurston out of the way, and I was trying to break Donny Anderson's leg, only I went too low and he hit me with his knee in the head. The score was already 35–10, and there was something like a minute and 50 seconds left in the game, and I just laid there. I was too embarrassed to get up. I said, 'I refuse. You want me to get off the field, you carry me off.'"

McGee had caught another touchdown pass, for 13 yards. Green Bay intercepted Dawson once and yielded all of 12 yards in the third period. The final score of 35–10 sure looked like the rout that answered the NFL's prayers.

"The Chiefs are a good team, but we wore 'em down," a relieved Lombardi said. "We had a little more personnel than they did. Dallas is a better team; I guess that's what you want me to say.

"The Chiefs are good, but not as good as the top teams in our league."

That would come, though. Very soon.

END OF AN ERA

After frostbite and frozen victory, the Packers were an aging, battered, and not particularly imposing NFL champion heading into the second AFL-NFL title game. More like survivors after edging Dallas in the Ice Bowl at Lambeau Field, a game won on Bart Starr's one-yard quarterback sneak in the final seconds.

One fan died of exposure during that frigid game, when the temperature was a record 13 below zero, with a wind chill of minus 46. Several players suffered frostbite, a painful and lasting reminder of how cruel the tundra can be, no matter how much you love football.

"I don't want this to sound trite, because it's not—it's attitude," Starr said of the Ice Bowl victory. "It's a mental thing. You put [the conditions] out of your mind and focus on what the purpose and what your objectives are. You have to push it away."

Push away the unbearable discomfort? Not even Lombardi's Packers could do that entirely. But they were better off than the Cowboys.

"We were freezing," said guard Jerry Kramer, whose block led Starr into the end zone for the winning touchdown. "They were dying."

Would there be a carryover into the matchup with the AFL champion Oakland Raiders in Miami's Orange Bowl?

The Raiders had no such agonizing experience in their 40–7 rout of Houston for Oakland's first AFL crown. Indeed, the superconfident Raiders were almost cocky heading into the meeting with the Packers.

"We were 13–1 during the season; we had no trouble with the Oilers [in the AFL championship game]," said guard Gene Upshaw, one of a handful of future Hall of Famers on the Oakland roster. "We had every right to believe we not only deserved to be there but that we would win."

A look at the comparative seasons and health of the teams would have indicated that the Raiders would be favored, but the Pack was a 13½-point choice. Green Bay's Hall of Fame running backs, Paul Hornung and Jim Taylor, were gone, and their replacements, Elijah Pitts and Jim Grabowski, got hurt during the season. Starr also had battled injuries.

But the outstanding offensive line and a powerhouse defense anchored the defending champions. And the Raiders, after all, were from the AFL.

Still, there was no backing down by Oakland—at least not at the outset.

"Those predictions—Oakland a two-touchdown underdog—are ridiculous," said Raiders quarterback Daryle Lamonica, the most prolific passer in pro football in 1967. "Green Bay is a great football team, there can be no doubt about that. We respect them. But we should have been undefeated this year. You're a good football team when you come close to winning 15 games in a row.

"This is a young, strong football team. It makes mistakes, but all year it proved it could overcome them."

Except against the Packers. Just as in the previous year's game with the Chiefs, the Pack would take a lead and not let the upstarts from the AFL come back.

Some differences from AFL-NFL I, though.

Attendance, for example: 75,546, the first in a steady run of Super Bowl sellouts. Rozelle had sworn after the embarrassment of the Los Angeles Coliseum that no future championship contest would have empty seats.

And one TV network: CBS. Bills quarterback Jack Kemp was imported to join Ray Scott and Pat Summerall in the broadcast booth, giving the game an AFL face on a network that telecast NFL games.

A slew of field goals, too: four by Green Bay's Don Chandler.

From an AFL perspective, some things were too, too similar to the previous year. An MVP performance by Starr, including long touchdown passes—McGee even caught another one. A huge defensive play by Green Bay, this one Herb Adderley returning an interception 60 yards for a touchdown.

Oakland's defenders, dubbed "Eleven Angry Men," could only be mad at themselves in the 33–14 Packers romp.

There could be no questioning the NFL's superiority now.

It also was the end of an era. Two actually, although only one would be so apparent in early 1968: soon after guiding the Packers to a third straight title and fifth in seven years, Lombardi resigned as coach. He would never coach another game for Green Bay.

The other era that was concluding? How about the NFL's dominance. All those AFL detractors were about to be silenced by a flamboyant quarterback with a golden arm and a charm to match.

VICTORY GUARANTEED

Super Bowl III would be the most important of the AFL-NFL matchups, regardless of the winner. Should the NFL representative triumph again, especially in a rout, the viability of such championships games would be severely questioned. And if the AFL team somehow managed to keep it close or, preposterously, win the thing, the upstart league would have the bona fides to make the merger valid.

In the establishment's corner were the rugged Baltimore Colts, 13–1 during the season and who had blitzed Cleveland into submission 34–0 for the NFL title. On the other side were the glamorous New York Jets, led by Joe Willie Namath and coached by Weeb Ewbank, who a decade earlier had led the Colts to two NFL crowns.

"The Colts were an 18-point favorite," recalled Gil Brandt, then the Cowboys' general manager, "and there were people there that predicted another 73–0 game."

Brandt referred to the Chicago Bears' beating of the Washington Redskins in the 1940 NFL championship game, the worst rout in league history.

There was some other predicting going on as well, which Namath foreshadowed with this comment after the Jets edged the Raiders 27–23 for the AFL title: "We can win this game," Namath said. "There are five better quarterbacks in the AFL than [National Football League most valuable player] Earl Morrall [of the Colts]."

Of course, Namath listed himself as one of the five.

"People couldn't believe he was saying those things," Jets publicist Frank Ramos recalled.

They would be even more incredulous with Namath's words a little while later.

Baltimore was coached by a young Don Shula, destined to become the winningest pro football coach and the only man to lead a perfect team (1972 Dolphins) to an NFL title. But the Colts were a veteran squad so talented that they could afford to let the great John Unitas sit behind Morrall as they reeled off win after win. Their defense was overwhelming, with four shutouts and 11 games allowing 10 points or fewer.

And they carried a grudge that grew bigger with every word they heard out of Jets camp.

"I have a lot of respect for Joe," said fearsome defensive end Bubba Smith. "He's an exceptional quarterback. But a football player who's real good doesn't have to talk. The Green Bay Packers were real champions. They never talked. They never had to. That's the way I visualize all champions, dignified and humble.

"All this Namath talk is going to fire us up."

Particularly after Broadway Joe went as far as he could verbally.

Speaking at a Miami Touchdown Club luncheon where he was being honored as player of the year, Namath approached the microphone just as a Colts fan in the audience yelled, "Hey, Namath, we're going to kick your ass."

Namath was startled, but not speechless.

"Whoa, wait a minute—you guys have been talking for two weeks now," Namath said, referring to anyone and everyone who bragged about the Colts' greatness. "I'm tired of hearing it."

Then Namath said, "I've got news for you. We're going to win the game. I guarantee it."

Namath later explained, "I didn't plan it. I never would have said it if that loudmouth hadn't popped off. I just shot back. We had a good team, but people were treating us like we didn't belong. I was fed up with it, and I guess it just came out."

It was something sports fans might have expected from Muhammad Ali, who had a habit of predicting the round in which his opponent would fall to the canvas. But while Namath was plenty outlandish, from the fur coats in his wardrobe and shaving cream commercials with Farrah Fawcett to the air of confidence he exuded—and that penetrated his teammates—Joe Willie had not particularly been a braggart.

Now this? And suddenly the AFL-NFL Championship Game in Miami was taking on a super air. Maybe it wouldn't be so competitive on the field, but it was getting plenty hot off of it.

Which was a good thing, just the spice needed.

"I'll tell you, that guarantee was probably one of the greatest things Joe could have done because the Colts were really pissed off," Jets center John Schmitt said. "They wanted to kill Namath and kill us. They wanted to eat us alive, and that had to throw them off their game."

According to future Hall of Fame tight end John Mackey, they were already off kilter.

"We laughed," the Colts' star said of Namath's boast. "We thought it was a joke. That was our problem. We had the wrong attitude. We started to believe we were 19-point favorites. We announced our victory party the Wednesday before the game and cut up the shares at the pregame meeting. Can you believe that?"

There were other indicators the Jets might have some advantages in the January 12, 1969, game at the Orange Bowl.

For one, they were relaxed and relishing their success and their surroundings while still staying focused on the task. Ewbank even allowed the wives to come along. It was a vacation for the wives, a good place to work out for the players.

"Weeb reasoned it would be very difficult to practice in New York on fields that were frozen," Ramos explained. "In Florida, we could make it like a boot camp and work the players hard and really get a lot of running in. And really work out the plays for the game.

"Besides, who better to watch over the players than their wives?"

When the players were watching film of the Colts, some of them admitted to getting giddy about the prospect of facing this supposedly awesome opponent.

Hours before Namath's prediction, during film study, tight end Pete Lammons called out, "Weeb, if you don't stop showing us film, we're going to get overconfident."

Added future Hall of Fame receiver Don Maynard, "We didn't think it was an upset [if the Jets won]. We thought we were going to win all along.

"But," Maynard added, "Joe did add a little fuel to the fire."

A little fuel? More like an atomic explosion.

The guarantee didn't only annoy the Colts. Ewbank was at first stunned, then angry.

"The only one it got to really bad was Weeb," Maynard said. "Boy, he was mad because he didn't ever want us to do anything to fire up the other team."

It bothered Namath that he'd gotten up Ewbank's ire.

"He was upset—very upset," Namath said. "And he was right because he wanted the Colts overconfident, and I had messed things up, it appeared."

The Jets also had some strategy in mind that could—and would—befuddle the Colts.

Ewbank had not one but two outstanding running backs in Matt Snell and Emerson Boozer. Throughout the season, while Namath was making most of the headlines, Snell and Boozer were triggering a potent running game.

The coach decided to use both Snell and Boozer on most downs against the Colts and to alternate their assignments. Baltimore's stud defenders—Bubba Smith, Billy Ray Smith, Fred Miller, Mike Curtis, and Jerry Logan—would not be able to key on one runner.

"Whoever was having a good day, we made a pact that everyone else was going to block for him," Snell told the *New York Daily News*. "I was going good that day, so we just kept running it and running it, and Booz kept blocking. He blocked all day and never complained."

Ewbank also feared that tackle Sam Walton could not handle Bubba Smith, the best defensive end in the game, a sack machine who would gladly break Namath to pieces if he got the opportunity. So he moved guard Dave Herman over to Walton's right-tackle spot, negating any film study Smith had done.

"Looking back on it, that was probably one of the greatest adjustments ever made in football—when coach Ewbank moved [Herman] from left guard to right tackle to block Bubba Smith," Maynard said. "Haystack [Herman] did a tremendous job. I don't think Bubba ever got to Joe all day, except maybe one time on a blitz he brushed him."

One more thing. Maynard, by far the Jets' best deep threat despite being an original Titan and their oldest receiver, was nursing a hamstring injury. Namath and Maynard suggested to Ewbank that very early in the game the quarterback air out a deep ball to the veteran, knowing that Maynard could go long on one route without jeopardizing his leg.

While the Jets didn't complete the throw, as Maynard said, "it got the Colts thinking they had to watch the deep ball." For most of the remainder of the game, Maynard drew double coverage, freeing George Sauer, Snell, and Lammons. Maynard didn't catch a ball—not one—yet he wasn't needed.

New York's almost carefree attitude carried directly into the game. So did the uptight environment for the Colts. In fact, it was noticeable from the stands.

Willie West, a former Jets defensive back who joined the expansion Dolphins in 1966 and was living in Miami, was at the Orange Bowl. From his seat, he recognized the differences in each team from the beginning.

"I remember that Baltimore had a tough time handling the Jets. I think they were shell-shocked, actually," West said. "You could see from the start of the game how their body language was. As the game proceeded, the Jets were doing so well, and all of a sudden Baltimore realized, 'We are going to have to play this game; we can't just show up and win.'

"It was very evident to me as a player watching from the stands to see those dynamics. Baltimore was shocked the Jets were right there with them from the outset. To me, it was clearly they were overconfident. You could see it in pregame warm-ups, even. They thought they could show up and the game would be over."

The game pretty much was over well before the final whistle but hardly in the manner the Colts, the rest of the NFL—or the rest of the nation—could have expected.

Namath, whose quick release was the envy of all quarterbacks, worked the short routes to Sauer, Snell, and Lammons, intermingled with the superb running game behind Herman, Schmitt, Winston Hill, and the rest of the formidable blocking unit.

The Jets' defense was opportunistic with four interceptions, three in the first half. One came on a tipped pass in the end zone that Randy Beverly corralled, prompting several Colts players to slam their helmets into the turf on their sideline. Another came when Morrall failed to see a wide-open Jimmy Orr on a flea-flicker, instead throwing for Jerry Hill and having Jim Hudson intercept the pass.

"It would've been 7–7 at the half," Orr said. "We had used that play in the second game of the season, Earl's second game with us, and we scored a touchdown in Atlanta. We hadn't run it since then. I was 37, 38 yards open."

The botched play was indicative of how Baltimore's offense failed—failed to make the key plays, failed to uphold the NFL tradition, just plain failed.

And the defense that was usually tough to penetrate wasn't much better.

Snell rushed 30 times for 121 yards and caught four passes for 40 more. His four-yard run with 5:57 remaining in the second quarter put the Jets on top 7–0.

Jim Turner kicked three field goals to make it 16–0, and a desperate Shula inserted Unitas, who guided the Colts to a fourth-quarter touchdown.

Hardly enough.

Final: Jets 16, Colts 7.

The lasting image from what is still called the biggest upset in pro football history is Namath trotting off the field, his index finger held high, signifying not only that the Jets were number 1 but also that the AFL was for real.

"There's a certain oneness you feel being part of a champion," Namath said. "Forever, not just the players as New York Jets, but as players from the AFL, could say that we did it.

"We did it!"

Not only had they shocked the football universe, but the Jets had reset the course of the sport as well.

The Cowboys' Brandt was one of the onlookers who was not so shocked that the Jets took charge early and pretty much had the game in hand by the fourth quarter. He knew what it all meant.

"No question that is the game that saved the league," he said. "Without that, I am not sure the merger would have worked out as well as it did.

"What it said was that AFL teams now had reached the point that they could compete with teams in the NFL. I think any time you are the underdog and have been for two years or three years, and all of a sudden start to get better and competitive, I think it creates more interest. Now, all of a sudden, you have got teams that can beat teams in the other league."

For all the joy on the AFL side—there wasn't a player, general manager, owner, or fan of the league who couldn't share in this victory—there was the crushing realization on the other side that the NFL's air of superiority had been snuffed.

Staunch AFL detractors would call the Jets' win a fluke. They would come down hard on Shula and his players for not being totally prepared, for underestimating Namath and the Jets, and for making bad decisions before kickoff and worse decisions after it.

But Rozelle knew better.

"Everybody from the NFL was so down in the wake of the game," said Joe Browne. "NFL guys looked at it like it was a disaster, but Pete, in between puffs on a cigarette, said, 'This is the best thing that could happen to us.'

"He reasoned that, number one, it got New York excited at a time when the Giants were not doing great, and New York always is a key market. Number two, he said many people had seen the AFL as an inferior product, the inferior of the two leagues. The NFL had won the first two Super Bowls. But now . . . we had some balance. It gave them great credibility."

And the AFL wasn't through making waves. Tidal waves.

UNDENIABLE EQUALS

A fluke. Pure luck. Won't ever happen again.

The authenticity of the Jets' upset of the Colts began being questioned, oh, maybe 30 minutes after it happened. The NFL excuse machine was at full throttle.

And everyone in the AFL knew that there was only one way to fully legitimatize what Joe Willie and the Jets had done: do it again, even more emphatically.

Despite the victory over the Colts, the AFL was still the underdog in Super Bowl competition. Dawson remembered that there was some doubt that still lingered from the start of the AFL.

Dawson remembered a comment from Paul Brown when the quarterback was with the Cleveland Browns. Brown told his players that there was a new league starting up, "but don't pay any attention, it will never last."

Brown said that the new league was run by "sons of rich guys" who didn't know anything about football. Ironically, Brown later became an AFL owner himself when he started up the Cincinnati Bengals in the late 1960s.

While it was true that the AFL had come a long way, it still needed to prove itself in another big game between the leagues to establish any kind of equality in the public mind.

This was reflected in the betting line in Super Bowl IV—the Minnesota Vikings were installed as 12½-point favorites over Dawson's Chiefs.

The Vikings, led by their rugged Purple People Eaters defense, had hammered out a 12–2 record. The Vikings had held 10 opponents to 10 points or fewer—including a 27–7 victory over Cleveland for the NFL championship.

The Chiefs were no slouches—they had gone 11–3 and beaten the previous two AFL champions to get to Super Bowl IV.

"We had a heck of a football team at that time, a big football team," Steadman reasoned. "We were one of the biggest teams in the league. We were a much bigger, stronger team than Minneapolis. But nobody gave us a chance to win the game against the Purple People Eaters."

The full-fledged merger between the leagues was planned for the 1970 season. That included moving three franchises to what would become the AFC, regular interconference play, and everyone competing under the NFL banner with Rozelle as commissioner. So this would be the final grudge match between the upstarts and the establishment. It also was the first Super Bowl hosted by New Orleans, and a festive atmosphere accompanied the game.

But for the Chiefs, it was all business. They understood how critical it was to repeat the performance of the Jets, not their own showing in Super Bowl I.

"When the Jets won Super Bowl III, they won it for us, too, for the whole league. It got us some positive notoriety," Dawson said. "With us against the Vikings, we were again big underdogs. We hadn't seen the Vikings that year, but we knew they had one hell of a year. They had only given up four touchdowns rushing that year and outscored their opponents almost three to one, so they were on a roll."

As for his own team, Dawson felt the Chiefs were "the most talented AFL team ever."

The night before the Super Bowl, Dawson and star safety Johnny Robinson were discussing the matchup. Robinson had been concentrating solely on Minnesota's offense, led by former Canadian Football League quarterback Joe Kapp, receiver Gene Washington, and a power running game behind a staunch but not particularly large offensive line.

When Robinson asked Dawson how the Chiefs would fare against the Purple People Eaters, the quarterback responded presciently, "John, Hank has put together a game plan utilizing our strengths against their weaknesses. We are going to score some points."

And Robinson responded, "We might shut them out."

Sound familiar? Weren't the Jets speaking in the same confident tones the previous year? Why were the Chiefs so self-assured?

Consider:

—Kansas City was the more experienced team in such situations.

—The Chiefs were more skilled than three years earlier, having added the likes of linebackers Willie Lanier and Jim Lynch and cornerback James Marsalis and placekicker Jan Stenerud.

—They were very balanced on offense and defense and had excellent special teams.

—They were more battle tested, with a tougher route to the Super Bowl.

What did that route look like?

"Think what the Chiefs did that year, going 11–3," Dawson said. "Then we have to go to New York, the defending Super Bowl champs, and play them at Shea Stadium in the playoffs.

"The wind was a real factor, and it was frigid, and it was a battle. The big thing I remember as I was warming up with Fred Arbanas, our tight end who had lost sight in one eye, the wind would catch the ball and bounce it all over the place. He said he was stopping to go get one of the linemen over to catch the ball.

"'I lost one eye, and I am not losing the other,'" he said.

With the winds swirling—Shea Stadium was open ended, and the cold breezes blew in off Flushing Bay even during the Mets' baseball season—many passes by Namath and Dawson would die a quick death, plummeting into the dirt.

It was not the offense that would carry the Chiefs on this icy day but the superb defense.

In the fourth quarter, Kansas City led 6–3 but a pass interference call in the end zone put the ball at the 1. The Jets ran Snell and gained nothing on first down. Same thing for Bill Mathis on second down.

On third down, Namath tried a bootleg, and Lynch wasn't fooled. Namath threw away the ball, and the Jets settled for a field goal.

The game was tied 6–6.

"While this is going on," Dawson recalled, "I'm sitting on the bench next to Otis Taylor. He is diagramming a play on the sideline."

The play that Taylor conjured up involved having both wide receivers on the same side, with the tight end on the opposite side.

"So Otis says, 'You know when we line up in that, they are anticipating it. So they have the safety on me. If we go on a quick count, and I can get a good release, the safety has to cover me man to man, and if you can hold the other safety, I can make a move, and I think we can get it down the field."

As Dawson and the Chiefs took the field after the Jets' field goal, Otis asked the quarterback, "You thinking about calling the play right now?"

Dawson was.

And it worked like a charm.

"He was right on the coverage," Dawson said. "I knew I had to get a tight release and not let the wind get hold of it. I did, and when I looked, I thought I overthrew it. But Otis had other gears. Otis was one of the first big guys with a 4.4 or 4.5 sprinter's speed and was a great athlete.

"Anyway, Otis got free . . . and made the catch for 61 yards, got the ball down to the 19. On the next play, I hit Gloster Richardson for the touchdown."

Final: Chiefs 13, Jets 6.

And it was on to Oakland for an AFL title showdown with Kansas City's archrival.

Al Davis "relished" the opportunity to "put one on the Chiefs." In just a few years, he'd turned around one of the AFL's most dismal franchises, and the Raiders had usurped the Chiefs as the Western Division's dominant team.

So nobody would enjoy the beating that the Raiders were going "to put on the Chiefs" more than Oakland's owner.

"We're respectful of anyone we play, but we also know how well we have played all season," Davis said. "We won 12 [games], we lost only one, and we beat them twice. So who the hell is going to tell us we're not ready to be [AFL] champions?"

Well, the Chiefs, that's who. And they were the ones who planned to relish victory in the final pure-AFL game ever.

"The Raiders had been to the Super Bowl two years before, they had beaten us twice, and they were so confident that they had packed their bags for New Orleans and stashed their luggage in an area where they could get it after the game and head to the airplane," Dawson said. "There was only one week that year between the championship game and the Super Bowl.

"Their parking area for their cars when they drove to the game was near where the buses are. After we beat them, they had to walk with their baggage in hand past us to put them in the car trunks to head back home. I never let them forget that when I would see Raiders players after that.

"But at that time, no, we didn't [razz them]. We were too exhausted."

What had exhausted them? A 17–7 win for their record third AFL title as the Chiefs' defense sacked Lamonica and George Blanda four times, picked off three passes, and overcame four lost fumbles.

An ugly victory? Artistically, perhaps. Physically, definitely. Emotionally, it was a beauty for Hunt's guys.

"That win over the Raiders in what turned out to be the last game for the league, yes, that was very memorable and very satisfying that we won it," Hunt once said, noting that his team wore a patch on the jersey reading "AFL-10." "To represent the league in that Super Bowl, the last time any AFL team would be in it, was very special for the Chiefs."

To make it truly special, though, they needed to win it. Indeed, it can be argued that the Chiefs had more pressure on them than any previous AFL Super Bowl representative. In the first championship game between the leagues, Green Bay had all the stress as it defended the establishment's superiority. Same thing in the 1969 game for the Baltimore Colts.

The Jets could approach their meeting with the Colts in a carefree (if cocky) manner. But after they handled the Colts, the chore of validating that victory fell squarely on the Chiefs.

Plus, the Vikings would arrive in a foul mood, eager to extinguish the AFL's flame before it completely burned down the NFL's tower of power.

But the Vikings had some preparation issues.

"It's hard to plan for a team when you've only seen them on three films," coach Bud Grant said. "We've got nine years of Bart Starr on film. All we know about the Chiefs is that their style is similar to that of the Dallas Cowboys."

If that was all the Vikings knew, they weren't doing their homework because the Chiefs knew plenty about their opponent.

Such as how Minnesota's cornerbacks played deep. And how the Vikings' special teams didn't measure up to Kansas City's. And how the Chiefs were faster at most positions.

And most notably to Stram, how the Kansas City defense was going to be too big and too physical for the Vikings.

"I didn't think their line could handle Buck [Buchanan] and Curley [Culp] and our guys up front," Stram said.

Stram threw in yet another wrinkle to the Chiefs' game plan that would befuddle Minnesota.

"One part of the game plan that worked very well was the end-around," Dawson said. "Frank Pitts's speed and the fact they were a team that would really flow with the first direction of the backs made it work.

"David Hill, our right tackle, did a heck of a job of faking out Carl Eller like it would be a run the other way and then cutting him. He's the key guy on the blocks. And we had the guards pulling around and always went on a quick count. Eller took the bait on the fake by the tackle going down the field and peeling back, and Hill was able to make a block.

"That gave them something else to worry about."

It seemed that the Chiefs' biggest worries came during the buildup to the game. On Tuesday, NBC reported on its national news that a federal gambling investigation would summon Dawson to Detroit and that the quarterback could be implicated in the case. A gambler named Donald Dawson, no relation to Len, was at the center of the investigation, and Donald Dawson had made phone calls to the football player in the past.

The Chiefs' Dawson was stunned by the reports.

"Somebody was trying to make a name for himself in Detroit and named about 12 guys [involved with a bookie or betting], and mine was one of them," Dawson said. "I happened to be the starting quarterback in the Super Bowl, and so that got attention. My name was one of many, including Joe Namath.

"I knew the guy they were talking about and had not seen him in a year. They were getting info from the phone calls he made, and he made a couple to me that year. One was when I injured my knee—he called to check and see how I was. The other was my father passed away before the Jets game in November, and he called to offer condolences.

"If we had not been there [to the Super Bowl] before, it probably would have been a distraction. I still remember Fred Arbanas, who is from Detroit, said, 'What the hell, I am from Detroit, I am supposed to get all the notoriety from Detroit.'

"It was all a bunch of crap, and it was difficult on the family and friends."

One way to ease the stress: win the game.

Exactly what the Chiefs did.

Kansas City moved the ball enough to get into long field goal range, and Jan Stenerud booted a 48-yarder for a 3–0 lead. That was the first piece of intimidation.

"I looked over to Minnesota's sideline, and they looked like they were in shock—their kicker did not have that range," Dawson noted. "What that meant to them was, 'We can't let these guys past midfield.'"

But the Chiefs got past midfield often enough to build a 16–0 halftime edge, befuddling the Vikings with a sharp short-passing style, with the end-arounds to Pitts, with double-team blocking on fearsome defensive end Eller, and with Stenerud's leg.

Plus an overwhelming defense that Kapp couldn't solve.

And when the Vikings finally got a touchdown in the third period, the Chiefs applied the coup de grâce to the last AFL-NFL Championship Game.

Down 16–7, the Vikings got ultra-aggressive on defense, leading to their demise. Dawson dropped back, turned to his right, and threw to Taylor.

"That little old hitch pass to Otis Taylor was the biggest play, of course. We got lucky and called it at the most opportune time in the third quarter," Dawson said. "They didn't blitz much; they had confidence they could get pressure with their front people. On that play, though, they had an all-out blitz.

"We went on a quick count, and they were trying to camouflage the blitz. Because of the quick count, I was able to get it to Otis, and he broke the tackle by [Earsell] Mackbee, and he went down the sideline for 46 yards, and that was the game."

Pretty much.

Dawson was chosen the most valuable player following the Chiefs' 23–7 win, but he—and everyone else—knew this was a collaborative effort.

"The Kansas City defensive line resembled a redwood forest," Kapp said. "I don't remember that one individual stood out—they were all very active. We went into the game wanting to run the ball, and they were able to take it all away with great defensive play. We couldn't come up with the big play when we wanted to."

Added safety Karl Kassulke, "We made more mental mistakes in one game than we did in one season."

That comment, however, did not give proper credit to the Chiefs and to how far the AFL had come in 10 years: truly the "little league that could."

"After the Jets beat Baltimore," Dawson noted, "people said it was a fluke. After we dominated Minnesota, they could no longer call it a fluke. They had to recognize the talent in the AFL."

Epilogue: The Legacy

Through the years, there have been several little leagues that couldn't. The World Football League (WFL) tried to challenge the NFL in the 1970s, perhaps buoyed by what the AFL achieved.

The WFL flopped.

In the 1980s, the United States Football League (USFL), backed by some deep-pocketed owners and playing in several showcase stadiums, took up the fight. Like the WFL, the USFL started out with a spring/summer schedule and attracted players who eventually would become stars in the big time: Reggie White, Doug Flutie, and Steve Young, for instance.

And the USFL even won a lawsuit against the NFL. It shouldn't have bothered. The USFL was awarded the whopping sum of $3 for its trouble. Then it went away for good.

In 2009, the United Football League (UFL) held its premier season with four teams, hoping to double and then triple in size. It claimed to be a complement to the NFL and played a two-month schedule in the midst of the established league's season. Eventually, UFL executives might begin thinking big, too.

But nothing compares to what the AFL achieved in its 10 seasons.

"Because of the type owners we had, the majority of them were very successful in other businesses, and they were great owners to the players," said Lance Alworth, the first AFL player elected to the Hall of Fame after a scintillating career beating defenses as San Diego's top receiver. "More than anything, they had credibility. Barron Hilton owned the Chargers, and you can't get any more credible than that. Buffalo owner Ralph Wilson, he's in the Hall of Fame. All those guys were so successful in whatever they did and chose really good people to run their football teams.

"They were not going to be run out by the NFL or by anyone else. When they made up their minds to do this, they had the financial backing and backing in their cities, and they backed up each other."

They also spread the pro football gospel. At a time when baseball still ruled the sporting landscape, the AFL helped extend the boundaries for a game that, until the 1960s, was more popular on the college level.

With teams in such outposts as Houston, Denver, Kansas City, San Diego, and Dallas, the AFL was bringing the pro game to uncharted territories where the college brand—or even hockey—drew far more headlines.

"By increasing the number of markets where pro football was played in the 1960s, the AFL in that decade helped move our sport ahead of baseball as the fans' favorite," said longtime NFL executive Joe Browne. "We have been widening the gap over all sports since that time."

That gap has become a canyon because the AFL succeeded, because it forged a merger—and because the AFL was more open-minded than its established foe. The AFL heavily recruited African American players, particularly from the predominantly black schools throughout the South and Southwest.

Plus, the AFL's significant presence on television—Sundays in the 1960s often meant four TV games in most markets, two from each league—led to the creation of stars and sages. From the colorful (Joe Namath and Ben Davidson) to the cunning (Hank Stram and Sid Gillman), from the brawny (Buck Buchanan and Billy Shaw) to Bambi (Lance Alworth), from the powerful (Jim Nance and Cookie Gilchrist) to the explosive (Abner Haynes and Speedy Duncan) to the clever (Fred Biletnikoff and Len Dawson), the AFL was a trendsetter.

A trendsetter on and off the field.

"The AFL made it because the NFL did not take them seriously, did not think they would last," Hall of Fame tackle Ron Mix said. "So they allowed about 70 percent of the best players in the first four years to go to the new league. They didn't want to compete with them financially. And they didn't begin to take the league seriously until Joe Namath signed."

Eventually, though, everyone in the NFL recognized how serious their plight would be without peace. In the decades since, the NFL, now with 32 franchises, avoided bidding wars and rival upstarts while becoming an $8 billion business.

And, remember, without the AFL, there would be no grand American quasi-holiday, Super Sunday. If anything is a lasting legacy, that is.

"I'm not sure we ever imagined the Super Bowl would become so big so soon," Lamar Hunt once said. "I guess it's a sign of how successful we were."

"We" meaning the not-so Foolish Club. More like the Brilliant Bunch.

Index